Chloe Courtney in association with Neil McPherson
for the Finborough Theatre presents

The world premiere

P'YONGYANG
by In-Sook Chappell

D1377602

FINBOROUGH | THEATRE

First performed at the Finborough Theatre: Tuesday, 5 January 2016

P'YONGYANG

by In-Sook Chappell

Cast in order of speaking

Yeon Eun Mi	**Anna Leong Brophy**
Park Chi Soo	**Chris Lew Kum Hoi**
Mrs Park, Min, Waitress	**Lourdes Faberes**
Mr Park, The Producer	**Daniel York**

Act One takes place at the end of the 1980s.
Act Two takes place through the 1990s.
Act Three takes place in summer 2011.

The performance lasts approximately ninety minutes.
There will be no interval.

Director	**Chelsea Walker**
Designer	**Max Dorey**
Lighting Designer	**Jamie Platt**
Sound Designer and Composer	**Harry Blake**
Movement Director	**Jenny Ogilvie**
Costume and Props Supervisor	**Katharine Davies-Herbst**
Assistant Director	**Lakesha Arie-Angelo**

Our patrons are respectfully reminded that, in this intimate theatre, any noise such as rustling programmes, talking or the ringing of mobile phones may distract the actors and your fellow audience-members.

We regret there is no admittance or re-admittance to the auditorium whilst the performance is in progress.

Lourdes Faberes | Mrs Park, Min, Waitress

Theatre includes *Hidden* (Royal Court Theatre), *Golden Child* (New Diorama Theatre), *La Boheme*, *Orphée* (Royal Opera House, Covent Garden), *Still* (Theatre503), *Hungry Ghosts* (Orange Tree Theatre, Richmond), *One Day, Twenty Years* (The Young Vic), *Cruel and Tender* (The Young Vic, Chichester Festival Theatre and Bouffes de Nord, Paris) and *A Funny Thing Happened on the Way to the Forum* (Theatre Royal York).

Film includes *The Heart of the Forest*, *Mother of Pearl*, *Someone You Love*, *Balsa Wood*, *Room 304*, *Spread* and *State of Play*.

Television includes *Grantchester*, *Safelight 19*, *Holby City*, *Law and Order UK*, *The Thai Bride* and *New Tricks*.

Anna Leong Brophy | Yeon Eun Mi

Theatre includes *Pitcairn* (Chichester Festival Theatre and Shakespeare's Globe), *Yeh Shen* (Yellow Earth), *How to Waste Money on Mere Happiness* (New Diorama Theatre), *The Art of Fugue* (Soho Theatre), *Cure* (Underbelly, Edinburgh), *Shelf Life* (Theatre Delicatessen) and *BattleActs* (Roundhouse).

Film includes *The Conversations*, *GBH*, *The Diana Clone* and *Malaya: A Forgotten War*.

Chris Lew Kum Hoi | Park Chi Soo

Theatre includes *A Midsummer Night's Dream*, *A Life of Galileo*, *Boris Godunov*, *The Orphan of Zhao* (Royal Shakespeare Company), *The World of Extreme Happiness* (National Theatre), *Peter Pan* (Open Air Theatre, Regent's Park), *James and the Giant Peach* (West Yorkshire Playhouse) and *Fox Attack* (National Theatre of Scotland).

Television and Film includes *War Machine* and *Doctor Who*.

Daniel York | Mr Park, The Producer

Productions at the Finborough Theatre include *Our American Cousin*, *The Wallace* and *We Know Where You Live*.

Theatre includes *The World Of Extreme Happiness* (National Theatre), *The Merchant Of Venice*, *The Country Wife*, *Moby Dick* (Royal Shakespeare Company), *The Importance Of Being Earnest*, *The Birds* (International Tour), *Animal Farm* (Theatre Royal, Hobart, Tasmania), *Boeing Boeing* (Drama Centre Theatre, Singapore), *Turandot* (Hampstead Theatre), *Branded* (The Old Vic), *Five Tanks* (Hackney Empire), *The Good Woman Of Setzuan* (Haymarket Theatre, Leicester), *In The Bag* (Traverse Theatre, Edinburgh), *Tartuffe* (Haymarket Theatre, Basingstoke), *The Changeling* (Southwark Playhouse), *Sun Is Shining* (King's Head Theatre and 59E59 Theaters, New York City), *Romeo and Juliet* (Haymarket Theatre, Basingstoke), *Measure For Measure* (Library Theatre, Manchester), *Nativity* (Birmingham Rep), *Une Tempete* (Gate Theatre), *Kiss of the Spiderwoman*, *The Glass Menagerie* (Singapore Repertory Company), *The Magic Fundoshi* (Lyric Theatre, Hammersmith), *Hamlet* (Thelma Holt Productions) and *Porcelain* (Royal Court Theatre).

Film includes *Rogue Trader*, *The Beach*, *Doom*, *Act Of Grace* and *The Receptionist*.

Television includes *Whitechapel*, *Moving On*, *Waking the Dead*, *Casualty*, *Peggy Su!*, *Chambers*, *The Bill*, *Supper at Emmaus* and *A Fish Named Tao*.

Radio includes *Doggie's Nirvana*, *Romeo and Juliet*, *The Monkey King*, *Dead Lines*, *Say It With Flowers* and *The Inspector Chen Mysteries*.

In-Sook Chappell | Playwright

In-Sook Chappell was born in Korea but raised in England. She studied dance in New York at the Alvin Ailey School before moving into acting, and originally started writing between acting jobs.

Her first play *This Isn't Romance* won the Verity Bargate Award and was produced at the Soho Theatre, broadcast on BBC Radio 3 and commissioned as a screenplay by Film Four. Her other plays include *Tales of the Harrow Road* (Soho Theatre).

Radio includes *Hong Kong by Night* (BBC Radio 4). She wrote and directed a short film, *Full*, and is currently working on another short film, *Kochebi*.

Chelsea Walker | Director

Productions at the Finborough Theatre include *Chicken Dust*

Trained at the Royal Central School of Speech and Drama with an MA in Advanced Theatre Practice and Oxford University.

Direction includes *Chicken Dust* (Curve Leicester), *Klippies* (Southwark Playhouse), *Lean* (Tristan Bates Theatre), *Bespoke* (Southwark Playhouse), *Ocean of Loneliness* (Lost Theatre), *Citizens* (Theatre503) and *Occupied* (Bad Host at the Bush Theatre).

Assistant Direction includes assisting Simon Godwin on *Routes* (Royal Court Theatre), *The Little Mermaid* (Bristol Old Vic) and *Candida* (Theatre Royal Bath) and Amelia Sears on *Brimstone and Treacle* (Arcola Theatre). Chelsea is currently a reader for the Susan Smith Blackburn Prize and Hampstead Theatre, and is co-directing Southwark Playhouse Young Company's 2016 show.

Max Dorey | Designer

Productions at the Finborough Theatre include *Black Jesus* and *Coolatully.*

Trained in Theatre Design at Bristol Old Vic Theatre School. In 2013, he was one of two trainee designers at the Royal Shakespeare Company, and was also a finalist for the Linbury Prize for Stage Design during which time he worked with the National Theatre of Scotland. He has assisted designers including Tom Piper, Michael Vale, Angela Davies, Chris Oram, Ultz and Paul Wills.

Recent designs include *No Villain* (Old Red Lion Theatre), *All the Little Lights* (Nottingham Playhouse), *And Then Come the Nightjars* for which he was nominated for an OffWestEnd Award (Theatre503 and Bristol Old Vic), *Orson's Shadow*, *Teddy* (Southwark Playhouse), *Animals* (Theatre503), *Lardo* (Old Red Lion Theatre), *Sleight and Hand* (Summerhall), *The School for Scandal* (Waterloo East Theatre), *Oedipus* (Blue Elephant Theatre), *The Duke in Darkness* and *Marguerite* (Tabard Theatre).

Jamie Platt | Lighting Designer

Productions at the Finborough Theatre include *Chicken Dust* and *We Know Where You Live.*

Trained at the Royal Welsh College of Music and Drama with a first class Honours degree In Lighting Design. He was nominated for an OffWestEnd Award in 2015, and in 2013 was the recipient of the Association of Lighting Designers' ETC Award and the Philip and Christine Carne Prize from the Royal Welsh College of Music and Drama.

Lighting Designs include *Closer to Heaven* (Union Theatre), *Klippies* (Southwark Playhouse), *And Now: The World!* (Derby Theatre and UK Tour), *Make/Believe* (V&A Museum), *Ring The Changes+* (Southbank Centre), *The Marriage of Figaro* (Kirklinton Hall, Carlisle and UK Tour), *Mahmud íle Yezida*, *BOY*, *Misbehaving*, *The Intruder*, *The Bald Prima Donna*, *The Red Helicopter* (Arcola Theatre), *One Thousand + 1*, *Fellini: Book of Dreams*, *AnneX*, *QuiXote*, *Due Saponette Rosse di Tritolo*, *BURN* (Fucecchio, Italy), *Romeo and Juliet* (Pleasance London), *MICROmegas* (Riverside Studios), *Grimm Tales* (John Lyon Theatre), *Arthur's Quest* (V45, Edinburgh), *The Children's Hour*, *Earthquakes in London*, *Arabian Nights* (Bute Theatre), *Once a Catholic*, *The Merchant of Venice* (Richard Burton Theatre), *Merrily We Roll Along*, *Honk!* and *Footloose* (Epsom Playhouse).

Associate Lighting Designs include *The Grit in the Oyster* (Sadler's Wells and World Tour), *The Measures Taken*, *All That Is Solid Melts Into Air* (Linbury Studio, Royal Opera House, and World Tour), *Our Big Land* (New Wolsey Theatre, Ipswich, and UK Tour) and *Don Giovanni* (West Road Concert Hall, Cambridge).

Harry Blake | Sound Designer and Composer

Harry Blake is an award-winning composer, lyricist and sound designer for film and live performance. He recently scored the British feature film *Making It*, currently in post-production, and is working on a new musical, *How to Stop Being Fat and Start Being Happy*, with playwright Jon Brittain, author of *Margaret Thatcher*, *Queen of Soho*.

Composition includes *Cyrano* (BBC Radio 4), *Bike* (Salisbury Playhouse), *The Future for Beginners*, (Wales Millennium Centre and Tour), *The Glass Supper* (Hampstead Theatre), *Once Upon a Christmas* (Look Left, Look Right), *The Love Girl and the Innocent* (Southwark Playhouse), *Perle* (Tobacco Factory and Soho Theatre), and *A Midsummer Night's Dream*, *Othello* and *Cyrano de Bergerac* (Grosvenor Park Open Air Theatre).

Harry is a winner of the Craig Barbour Award for Composition at the Soho Theatre, the Musical Theatre Network Award at the Edinburgh Festival 2014, and was recently made an Associate of the Royal Academy of Music (ARAM).

Jenny Ogilvie | Movement Director

Productions at the Finborough Theatre include *Somersaults* and *The Soft of Her Palm*.

Trained as a movement specialist at the Royal Central School of Speech and Drama, as an actor at Webber Douglas Academy of Dramatic Art and previously studied languages at Oxford University.

Movement Direction includes *Lucia di Lammermoor* (Buxton Opera Festival), *Little Revolution*, assisting Imogen Knight (Almeida Theatre), *The Seven Deadly Sins* (Welsh National Opera at Cardiff University), *Three Sisters* (Southwark Playhouse), *Knock Yourself Out* (Courtyard Theatre), *A Midsummer Night's Dream*, *Sweeney Todd* and *Paul Bunyan* workshops (Welsh National Opera Youth Opera), *Vernon God Little* (Guildford School of Acting), *Three Sisters*, *Swan Song* and *The Broken Heart* (which she also co-directed), *Richard III* and *Antony and Cleopatra* (all Royal Central School of Speech and Drama).

As an actor, Jenny has worked in film (*Another Mother's Son*, *A Cock and Bull Story*), on television in regular series such as *Grantchester*, *Silent Witness*, *Poirot* and *Doctors*; and on stage including work at the Royal Shakespeare Company, Birmingham Rep, West End and the Royal Exchange Theatre, Manchester, where she was nominated for the TMA Award for Best Performance in a Play for J. M. Barrie's *What Every Woman Knows*.

Katharine Davies-Herbst |
Costume and Props Supervisor

Trained at Wimbledon College of Art. She has a background in site specific and immersive theatre and is also a painter.

Lakesha Arie-Angelo | Assistant Director

Lakesha is a Resident Assistant Director, supported by The Richard Carne Trust, at the Finborough Theatre where she has assisted on *Treasure* and *Vibrant 2015 – A Festival of Finborough Playwrights*.

Direction includes *The Colored Museum* (Edric Hall). She is the Artistic Director and playwright of Pidgin Playhouse whose work includes a staged reading of *Sugar, Rum, Molasses* (The CLF Theatre at The Bussey Building). Stage Management includes *Love is Not Enough* (The CLF Theatre at The Bussey Building), *When Nobody's Looking* (ArtsDepot) and *Sarafina!* (Edison Theatre, St.Louis, USA). Lakesha is also an Assistant Tutor at Clean Break.

Production Acknowledgements

With thanks to James Hoare, Jihyun Park, Sylvia Park, Asia House, the Korean Information Centre, Yellow Earth, The Agency and special thanks to Southwark Playhouse and Tandem.

FINBOROUGH | THEATRE

VIBRANT NEW WRITING | UNIQUE **REDISCOVERIES**

118 Finborough Road, London SW10 9ED

admin@finboroughtheatre.co.uk | www.finboroughtheatre.co.uk

"A disproportionately valuable
component of the London theatre
ecology. Its programme combines
new writing and revivals, in selections
intelligent and audacious."
Financial Times

"The tiny but mighty Finborough…
one of the best batting averages of
any London company."
Ben Brantley, *The New York Times*

"The Finborough Theatre, under the
artistic direction of Neil McPherson,
has been earning a place on the
must-visit list with its eclectic, smartly
curated slate of new works and
neglected masterpieces." *Vogue*

Founded in 1980, the multi-award-
winning Finborough Theatre presents
plays and music theatre, concentrated
exclusively on vibrant new writing and
unique rediscoveries from the 19th and
20th centuries. Our programme is unique
– never presenting work that has been
seen anywhere in London during the
last 25 years. Behind the scenes, we
continue to discover and develop a new
generation of theatre makers – through
our Literary team, and our programmes
for both interns and Resident Assistant

Directors. Despite remaining completely
unsubsidised, the Finborough Theatre
has an unparalleled track record of
attracting the finest talent who go on to
become leading voices in British theatre.
Under Artistic Director Neil McPherson,
it has discovered some of the UK's most
exciting new playwrights including Laura
Wade, James Graham, Mike Bartlett, Jack
Thorne, Simon Vinnicombe, Alexandra
Wood, Nicholas de Jongh and Anders
Lustgarten; and directors including
Blanche McIntyre, Robert Hastie and
Sam Yates.

Artists working at the theatre in the 1980s
included Clive Barker, Rory Bremner, Nica
Burns, Kathy Burke, Ken Campbell, Jane
Horrocks and Claire Dowie. In the 1990s,
the Finborough Theatre first became
known for new writing including Naomi
Wallace's first play *The War Boys*; Rachel
Weisz in David Farr's *Neville Southall's
Washbag*; four plays by Anthony Neilson
including *Penetrator* and *The Censor*,
both of which transferred to the Royal
Court Theatre; and new plays by Richard
Bean, Lucinda Coxon, David Eldridge,
Tony Marchant and Mark Ravenhill.
New writing development included the
premieres of modern classics such as
Mark Ravenhill's *Shopping and F***king*,
Conor McPherson's *This Lime Tree
Bower*, Naomi Wallace's *Slaughter City*
and Martin McDonagh's *The Pillowman*.

Since 2000, new British plays have
included Laura Wade's London debut
Young Emma, commissioned for the
Finborough Theatre; two one-woman
shows by Miranda Hart; James Graham's
Albert's Boy with Victor Spinetti; Sarah
Grochala's *S27*; Peter Nichols' *Lingua
Franca*, which transferred Off-Broadway;
Dawn King's *Foxfinder*; and West
End transfers for Joy Wilkinson's *Fair*;
Nicholas de Jongh's *Plague Over
England*; and Jack Thorne's *Fanny and
Faggot*. The late Miriam Karlin made her
last stage appearance in *Many Roads to
Paradise* in 2008.

We have also produced our annual festival of new writing – *Vibrant – A Festival of Finborough Playwrights* annually since 2009.

UK premieres of foreign plays have included plays by Brad Fraser, Lanford Wilson, Larry Kramer, Tennessee Williams, the English premiere of Robert McLellan's Scots language classic, *Jamie the Saxt*; and three West End transfers – Frank McGuinness' *Gates of Gold* with William Gaunt and John Bennett; Joe DiPietro's *F***ing Men*; and Craig Higginson's *Dream of the Dog* with Dame Janet Suzman.

Rediscoveries of neglected work – most commissioned by the Finborough Theatre – have included the first London revivals of Rolf Hochhuth's *Soldiers* and *The Representative*; both parts of Keith Dewhurst's *Lark Rise to Candleford*; *The Women's War*, an evening of original suffragette plays; *Etta Jenks* with Clarke Peters and Daniela Nardini; Noël Coward's first play, *The Rat Trap*; Charles Wood's *Jingo* with Susannah Harker; Emlyn Williams' *Accolade*; Lennox Robinson's *Drama at Inish* with Celia Imrie and Paul O'Grady; John Van Druten's *London Wall* which transferred to St James' Theatre; and J. B. Priestley's *Cornelius* which transferred to a sell out Off Broadway run in New York City.

Music Theatre has included the new (premieres from Grant Olding, Charles Miller, Michael John LaChuisa, Adam Guettel, Andrew Lippa, Paul Scott Goodman, and Adam Gwon's *Ordinary Days* which transferred to the West End) and the old (the UK premiere of Rodgers and Hammerstein's *State Fair* which also transferred to the West End), and the acclaimed 'Celebrating British Music Theatre' series.

The Finborough Theatre won *The Stage* Fringe Theatre of the Year Award in 2011, *London Theatre Reviews'* Empty Space Peter Brook Award in 2010 and 2012, the Empty Space Peter Brook Award's Dan Crawford Pub Theatre Award in 2005 and 2008, the Empty Space Peter Brook Mark Marvin Award in 2004, and swept the board with eight awards at the 2012 OffWestEnd Awards including Best Artistic Director and Best Director for the second year running. *Accolade* was named Best Fringe Show of 2011 by *Time Out*. It is the only unsubsidised theatre ever to be awarded the Channel 4 Playwrights Scheme nine times.

www.finboroughtheatre.co.uk

Artistic Director
Neil McPherson

Resident Designer | Deputy Chief Executive
Alex Marker

General Managers
Noa Nikolsky and **Doug Mackie**

Resident Producer
Luke Holbrook

Resident (with the support of The Richard Carne Trust
Amanda Castro

Playwrights in Residence
Bekah Brunstetter, **James Graham**, **Dawn King**, **Anders Lustgarten** and **Shamser Sinha** and **Chris Thompson**

Playwrights on Attachment
Steven Hevey, **Louise Monaghan** and **Carmen Nasr**

Literary Manager
Francis Grin

Deputy Literary Manager
Ben Lyon-Ross

Associate Designer
Phil Lindley

Resident Producer
Luke Holbrook

Resident Casting Directors
Lucy Casson, Georgia Fleury Reynolds and **Zoe Thorne**

Resident Assistant Directors
(with the support of The Richard Carne Trust)
Lakesha Arie-Angelo and **Anastasia Osei-Kuffour**

Board of Trustees
Felix Cassel, Davor Golub, Russell Levinson, Dr Matthew Linfoot, Rebecca Maltby and **Paul Webster**

And our many interns and volunteers.

The Finborough Theatre is a member of the Independent Theatre Council, the Society of Independent Theatres, Musical Theatre Network, The Friends of Brompton Cemetery and The Earl's Court Society
www.earlscourtsociety.org.uk

Supported by

Follow Us Online

Mailing
Email admin@finboroughtheatre.co.uk or give your details to our Box Office staff to join our free email list. If you would like to be sent a free season leaflet every three months, just include your postal address and postcode.

Feedback
We welcome your comments, complaints and suggestions. Write to Finborough Theatre, 118 Finborough Road, London SW10 9ED or email us at admin@finboroughtheatre.co.uk

Playscripts
Many of the Finborough Theatre's plays have been published and are on sale from our website.

Finborough Theatre T Shirts
Finborough Theatre T Shirts are on sale from the Box Office, available in Small and Medium £7.00.

Friends
The Finborough Theatre is a registered charity. We receive no public funding, and rely solely on the support of our audiences. Please do consider supporting us by becoming a member of our Friends of the Finborough Theatre scheme. There are various categories of Friends, each offering a wide range of benefits.

Smoking is not permitted in the auditorium and the use of cameras and recording equipment is strictly prohibited.

In accordance with the requirements of the Royal Borough of Kensington and Chelsea:

1. The public may leave at the end of the performance by all doors and such doors must at that time be kept open.

2. All gangways, corridors, staircases and external passageways intended for exit shall be left entirely free from obstruction whether permanent or temporary.

3. Persons shall not be permitted to stand or sit in any of the gangways intercepting the seating or to sit in any of the other gangways.

The Finborough Theatre is licensed by the Royal Borough of Kensington and Chelsea to The Steam Industry, a registered charity and a company limited by guarantee. Registered in England and Wales no. 3448268. Registered Charity no. 1071304. Registered Office: 118 Finborough Road, London SW10 9ED. The Steam Industry is under the overall Artistic Direction of Phil Willmott. www.philwillmott.co.uk

P'YONGYANG

In-Sook Chappell

P'YONGYANG

OBERON BOOKS
LONDON

WWW.OBERONBOOKS.COM

First published in 2016 by Oberon Books Ltd
521 Caledonian Road, London N7 9RH
Tel: +44 (0) 20 7607 3637 / Fax: +44 (0) 20 7607 3629
e-mail: info@oberonbooks.com
www.oberonbooks.com

A catalogue record for this book is available from the British
Library.

PB ISBN: 9781783193332
E ISBN: 9781783193349

Cover: Photo by Eric Lafforgue / Image by CGC

Printed and bound by Marston Book Services, Didcot.
eBook conversion by CPI Group (UK) Ltd, Croydon, CR0 4YY.

Visit www.oberonbooks.com to read more about all our books
and to buy them. You will also find features, author interviews and
news of any author events, and you can sign up for e-newsletters
so that you're always first to hear about our new releases.

Characters

Park Chi Soo, male

Yeon Eun Mi, female

Mr Park

Mrs Park

The Producer

Min

Waitress

The play can be performed by a cast of 4 actors.

The play should be performed in English without accents.
When Korean words and phrases are used
they should be pronounced correctly.

Act 1 takes place at the end of the 80s.
Act 2 takes place through the 90s.
Act 3 takes place in summer 2011.

For the people of North Korea

PROLOGUE

The cast stand onstage in a geometrically perfect formation. CHI SOO, fifteen, and EUN MI, fifteen, both wear school uniform: royal blue trousers and a knee length skirt, white shirts and red knotted scarves. They wear this throughout Act 1.

The music swells and they start to sing the patriotic song.

CAST: Let morning shine on all this land over the
        rivers and mountains,
        Three thousand li full of silver and gold,
        This is my beautiful fatherland,
        A five millennia long history,
        Brought up in a brilliant culture,
        The glory of a wise people,
        Let us glorify it forever.

They sing their hearts out, full of passion, with an almost religious fervour. Towards the end tears come to their eyes, they shake with emotion.

CAST: Embracing Baekdu mountain,
        Nest for the spirit of labour,
        The firm will, bonded with truth,
        Will go forth to all the world.
        The country established by the people
        Breasting the waves with a soaring strength,
        This rich and strong Korea,
        Let us glorify it forever.

They salute, right arm thrown into the air, the elbow bent. They turn and exit with military precision.

ACT ONE

SCENE ONE

CHI SOO stands outside the culture hall, an enormous portrait of Kim Il Sung covers it's exterior. CHI SOO is tall, handsome and confident. EUN MI watches him, she is awkward with bad posture.

EUN MI: *(Softly.)* Excuse me.

CHI SOO doesn't notice her.

EUN MI: Excuse me.

He doesn't notice her. EUN MI pulls together all her courage and speaks much louder than she was intending.

EUN MI: Chi Soo.

He turns and looks at her.

CHI SOO: Do I know you?

EUN MI: … I'm in your maths class. I sit behind you.

CHI SOO: Oh right.

EUN MI: But no … you don't know me.

CHI SOO: But you know who I am?

EUN MI: Everyone knows who you are.

CHI SOO smiles.

EUN MI: I was cheering for you last week. That goal you scored … I don't know anything about football but even I could see that it was something special.

CHI SOO: Thanks. I'm a striker. That's what I'm supposed to do, score.

EUN MI: Yes and it should have been three.

CHI SOO looks at her.

EUN MI: Not that … No … it was bad luck.

CHI SOO: Musan's defence is really strong.

EUN MI: I just meant it was a great effort and we should have won.

CHI SOO looks at her.

EUN MI: You … your goal made me proud to be from Komusan.

CHI SOO: What's your name?

EUN MI: Eun Mi.

CHI SOO: Are you going to see the film?

EUN MI: I hope so. That's why … I was wondering if you might have a spare ticket? I have money I can buy it from you.

EUN MI shifts from foot to foot. CHI SOO notices her rubber boots.

CHI SOO: Sorry I don't. I'm waiting for someone.

EUN MI looks disappointed. CHI SOO compares her boots to his worn canvas shoes.

CHI SOO: Nice boots.

EUN MI: My mother got them for me, she got the last pair, they're a bit tight.

CHI SOO: She must be important.

EUN MI: She runs the inminban in our area, is a devoted member of the Worker's Party.

CHI SOO: … What does your father do?

EUN MI: He used to work for the government.

CHI SOO looks impressed, glances around.

EUN MI: Are you waiting for Lee Sun Hee?

CHI SOO: Yes.

EUN MI: She's very beautiful.

CHI SOO: Yes she is.

EUN MI looks at him strangely.

EUN MI: Everyone says she will be chosen by Division 5 of the Central Worker's Party.

CHI SOO looks blank.

EUN MI: They look for girls with outstanding talent or exceptional beauty to attend upon the Great Leader and the Dear Leader. Hardly anyone gets picked, only the tallest, the most gorgeous.

CHI SOO: What happens if they choose you?

EUN MI: You have special training, then you get sent to one of our Father's many palaces. The only thing is … you're never allowed to go home again.

CHI SOO: Why?

EUN MI: I don't know. But your family is showered with expensive gifts. My mother wants me to try but … I don't think I'll make it.

CHI SOO: If you did, what would you have to do?

EUN MI: I'm not sure, maybe be a secretary or a maid. There's no real point in me thinking about it because … I don't look like Sun Hee.

CHI SOO: No … She's very … ambitious.

EUN MI: So am I … For the good of our country, for the collective.

CHI SOO: Me too.

EUN MI: Are you applying to high schools?

CHI SOO: Yes.

EUN MI: Which ones?

CHI SOO: The North Hamgyong School for the Performing Arts.

EUN MI: The NHSPA?

CHI SOO: Yes.

EUN MI: That's the hardest one to get into. Thirty people audition for every place.

CHI SOO: May as well aim high.

EUN MI nods, looks at him.

EUN MI: I saw you in the school play. You were …
You stood out. You were great.

CHI SOO beams.

EUN MI: Now I sound like a mad fan.

CHI SOO: That's alright. Acting makes me happy, even more than football. I like to imagine …

EUN MI: Sounds dangerous.

CHI SOO looks at her.

CHI SOO: You're funny.

EUN MI: Funny haha or funny peculiar?

CHI SOO: Funny haha. Do you know what the time is?

EUN MI: It must have been around five when I got here.

CHI SOO looks around for Sun Hee.

EUN MI: Oh Mee Ran's amazing. She's my favourite actress.

CHI SOO: Why?

EUN MI: Everything she does is simple, truthful. She really feels it and you can see her thoughts on her face even when there are no words.

CHI SOO: She won the best actress award at the P'yongyang Film Festival.

EUN MI: I know. That's why they've programmed this season. She plays the sort of characters who are sometimes overlooked because they aren't as obvious or loud as other women. She always has a quiet dignity and inner strength.

CHI SOO looks at her.

CHI SOO: That's the writer not her.

EUN MI: No. It's her. No one cares about the writer.

CHI SOO: I do. I admire Lee Chun Goo.

EUN MI: Who?

CHI SOO: He wrote this film. It's an incredible story.

EUN MI: Tell me, as I won't get to see it.

CHI SOO looks around for Sun Hee.

CHI SOO: It's a true story, based on the life of Han Soon Hee. Oh Mee Ran plays a wife and mother whose husband is killed fighting the South. After his death, she realizes her life is meaningless and that only work has worth. She turns her grief into something useful, a mountain of rice. She devotes herself to farming for the collective good and is named a hard working heroine.

Pause.

CHI SOO: A film starts with a script. It starts in the mind of a writer.

EUN MI: And you like to imagine.

CHI SOO: Exactly. I imagine films in my head. I can go anywhere in my head.

EUN MI: And that's what you want to do?

CHI SOO: Yeah. After being a film star.

EUN MI looks at him and giggles.

CHI SOO: Why not? I'm tall, I've got the right look.

CHI SOO strikes a pose, squints and stares into the distance towards a glorious future. They both laugh.

EUN MI: Everyone's gone in.

CHI SOO puts his hand in his pocket, takes out a ticket and gives it to EUN MI.

CHI SOO: You may as well have this.

EUN MI: But what about …?

CHI SOO: I don't want to miss the beginning because I'm waiting around for her.

EUN MI snatches the ticket before he changes his mind.

EUN MI: Thank you.

CHI SOO: You'll have to sit next to me. I hope you don't mind.

EUN MI: No … no that's fine.

CHI SOO glances around, doesn't want to be seen with EUN MI.

CHI SOO: Come on then.

They walk into the culture hall together.

SCENE TWO

A corridor in a run down institutional building. Eun Mi wears red lipstick, she sings 'The Night of P'yongyang City', a romantic popular song.

CHI SOO enters, he has greased back his hair, he stands watching her. EUN MI comes to the end of her song.

CHI SOO: You've got a good voice.

EUN MI: Thanks.

CHI SOO leans coolly against the wall.

EUN MI: And thank you for the other evening.

CHI SOO glances quickly around.

CHI SOO: Oh that was nothing. Anyway you paid for the ticket remember.

EUN MI: It wasn't nothing. You don't understand how much it meant to me to see that film. It's been in my head ever since.

CHI SOO looks at her.

CHI SOO: I think you might be as crazy about the movies as I am.

EUN MI: Probably even more.

CHI SOO: Not possible.

They look at each other and smile.

EUN MI: Song or monologue?

CHI SOO: Monologue.

EUN MI: Which one?

CHI SOO: The brother from the *Flower Girl*.

EUN MI: That's a great film.

CHI SOO: Isn't it. Don't get me started on seventies cinema.

EUN MI: *Sea of Blood*.

CHI SOO: Groundbreaking. The cinematography …
             Why aren't more films shot in black and white?

EUN MI: I don't know.

EUN MI hums an arpeggio.

CHI SOO: Why didn't you say you were auditioning?

EUN MI: I probably won't get in.

CHI SOO: You should be a bit more positive.

EUN MI: And if I don't … I'll be devastated and I don't
             want people to ask and then … pity me. There's nothing
             worse than being pitied.

CHI SOO: I can imagine … I would hate it.

EUN MI: Aren't you nervous?

CHI SOO: … No.

EUN MI: What other schools are you applying for?

CHI SOO: Only this one.

EUN MI: But what if you don't get in?

CHI SOO shrugs.

CHI SOO: Why … do you have a back up plan?

EUN MI: I have four …

A loudspeaker crackles. EUN MI jumps in fright, stands petrified.

CHI SOO: I think you should remember to breathe.

EUN MI nods.

CHI SOO: Especially if you're going to sing. And maybe if
             you stood up straight?

EUN MI stands up straight, takes a deep breath.

CHI SOO: You're actually quite pretty.

EUN MI gets flustered.

CHI SOO: Imagine them without any clothes. Imagine
             them sitting in a row behind the table without any clothes.

EUN MI looks at him horrified.

15

CHI SOO: They'll be less scary that way.

EUN MI: Is that how you imagine a lot of people?

CHI SOO: Only pretty girls.

EUN MI looks at him wide eyed.

CHI SOO: I've got a spare ticket to the cinema on Sunday.

EUN MI: *A Broad Bellflower?*

CHI SOO: Yes, that's it. Oh Mee Ran's in it.

EUN MI: I know.

Pause.

EUN MI: How do you manage to get Sunday tickets?

CHI SOO: I'm friendly with the girl in the box office.

The loudspeaker crackles.

CHI SOO: Fancy coming with me?

EUN MI: Yes.

RECORDED
   VOICE: Candidate 23 we are ready for you.

EUN MI panics.

CHI SOO: You can do it.

EUN MI closes her eyes.

CHI SOO: Breathe.

EUN MI takes a deep breath.

CHI SOO: Imagine the best possible outcome.

EUN MI smiles.

CHI SOO: Can you see it?

EUN MI: Yes.

CHI SOO: Then it can happen.

EUN MI opens her eyes, stands up straight.

CHI SOO: Imagine … them naked.

EUN MI looks at him in shock, then she grins and walks into her audition. CHI SOO leans back against the wall. The sound of EUN MI starting her song, 'The Night of P'yongyang City'.

SCENE THREE

Outside the culture hall. CHI SOO and EUN MI walk out of the culture hall.

EUN MI: We were the last to leave.

CHI SOO: We're professionals, well we will be. We wanted to read through to the end of the credits.

EUN MI stands still, closes her eyes.

CHI SOO: Are you alright?

EUN MI nods.

CHI SOO: What are you doing?

EUN MI: I want to keep this feeling for a little while.

CHI SOO looks at her.

CHI SOO: I can't believe I never noticed you.

EUN MI opens her eyes.

EUN MI: No one notices me.

CHI SOO: You're as pretty as Oh Mee Ran.

EUN MI laughs.

EUN MI: Division 5 didn't think so.

CHI SOO: You didn't …?

EUN MI shakes her head.

EUN MI: They picked Sun Hee.

CHI SOO: I heard.

A street lamp turns itself on.

EUN MI: I wish life was like it is in films.

CHI SOO: Like the film we just saw?

EUN MI: Yes.

CHI SOO: It was tragic. They were kept apart and then she died.

EUN MI: Yes, but there was such feeling. You need some sadness or there's no depth.

CHI SOO: Maybe. In films. They were both orphans, each other's first love, they belonged together. I don't understand why she didn't tell her sister to fuck off.

EUN MI looks down.

CHI SOO: Sorry.

EUN MI: Do you have brothers or sisters?

CHI SOO: No.

EUN MI: Well then, you wouldn't understand.

Pause.

CHI SOO: What was your favourite scene?

EUN MI: When they meet again at the train station after five years. Yours?

CHI SOO: The same. 'How are you?'

EUN MI looks at him in confusion.

CHI SOO: 'How are you?' The character that Oh Mee Ran plays.

EUN MI: Oh … 'I knew you'd come back.'

CHI SOO: 'No. I'm just passing through on my way to the city … This is our last chance … Come with me.'

CHI SOO gets their cinema tickets out of his pocket shows them to her.

CHI SOO: 'Look. I bought your ticket too … I'll make you happy.'

EUN MI: 'I … will stay in my home village although it's poor. Home is home.'

CHI SOO: 'Home can be anywhere.'

EUN MI: 'No.'

CHI SOO tears up the tickets.

EUN MI: 'Your wandering life will never lead you to happiness.'

They look at each other, grin.

CHI SOO: Have you seen it before?

EUN MI: Three times. You?

CHI SOO: Twice. But why does it have to be a choice between true love or duty?

EUN MI: You're the writer. If there's no conflict where's the drama?

CHI SOO: And of course she chooses duty.

EUN MI: Of course. She's the heroine … Apparently Oh Mee Ran was so talented that the Dear Leader himself gave her private acting lessons. After that … she became our biggest star.

CHI SOO: Maybe one day he'll notice you, give you a private acting lesson … Can I walk you home?

EUN MI: No. You'd better not.

EUN MI reaches into her canvas bag, brings out a book, presents it to CHI SOO solemnly.

EUN MI: It's my favourite. I can lend it to you.

CHI SOO: *On the Art of Cinema.*

EUN MI: It's by the Dear Leader himself.

CHI SOO opens the book, reads aloud.

CHI SOO: 'The actor is an artist who contributes through his portrayal of a character,'

EUN MI joins in, she knows it off by heart.

CHI SOO &
EUN MI: 'to deepening people's understanding of life and to re-educating them in a revolutionary manner.'

They look at each other.

EUN MI: I've underlined a few passages.

CHI SOO: I can see.

Pause.

EUN MI: I should go.

CHI SOO: Five minutes.

EUN MI: Alright.

CHI SOO: Shall we sit?

EUN MI nods, they walk over to a bench sit down, a gap between them.

EUN MI: When do you think we'll hear?

CHI SOO: Soon.

EUN MI: It's awful isn't it, the waiting.

CHI SOO: Yes. I wonder if they already know?

EUN MI: They probably decided on the day. I guess then they had to do the background checks.

EUN MI looks at CHI SOO.

EUN MI: What if we don't get in?

CHI SOO: I promise … I won't pity you.

EUN MI: I'm being serious.

CHI SOO: If we don't get in we'll work harder, practise longer and try again next year … There's always a way to get what you want.

EUN MI: Sometimes you sound dangerously individualistic.

CHI SOO: Everything we want would benefit the state. You want to be an actress to inspire people to work harder, to be better communists.

EUN MI: Yes … You know what I'd like?

CHI SOO: Tell me.

EUN MI: If we both got in.

Their eyes catch.

EUN MI: And we both progressed to the University of Cinematic and Dramatic Arts in P'yongyang.

CHI SOO: We could go to P'yongyang together. Do you know anyone who's been?

EUN MI: My mother… She told me there's a hotel like a palace set on its own island in the middle of P'yongyang.

CHI SOO: An island in P'yongyang?

EUN MI: Yes. The floors are made of a special stone that shines and is so slippery it's like walking on ice and the lightshades hang down from the ceiling like jewels. There are lifts operated by men in uniform with white gloves.

CHI SOO: Is it very tall?

EUN MI: Very. On the forty-seventh floor is a circular restaurant and the walls are all glass. The best thing is that it revolves.

CHI SOO: Shit … sorry.

EUN MI: You sit at an elegant table with a white table cloth and fresh cut flowers looking out at the view. As it turns you can see the entire city spread out beneath you.

CHI SOO: Do you think the Great Leader and the Dear Leader eat there?

EUN MI: Probably. My mother says it's the finest restaurant in P'yongyang. We'll be close to them.

Pause.

CHI SOO: Yes. I'll take you there.

EUN MI: I'll wear a silk dress … What will we eat?

CHI SOO: Bulgogi and …

EUN MI: Naengmyeon, three different types of kimchi.

CHI SOO: Four different types of namul.

They look at each other.

CHI SOO: Where else will we go?

EUN MI: To openings at the Mansudae Art Studios.

CHI SOO: Yes, we'll mix with other artists.

EUN MI: Of course, they'll be our friends. We'll go to the theatre and the opera.

CHI SOO: Where will we live?

EUN MI: Near the film studios.

CHI SOO: We'll be working very long days.

EUN MI: We'll be acting together in films.

CHI SOO: And later … I'll write films for you.

They sit side by side. CHI SOO glances at her hand, resting flat on the bench, he reaches out.

CHI SOO: Can I?

EUN MI quickly looks around.

EUN MI: *(Softly.)* Yes.

CHI SOO gently takes EUN MI's hand.

EUN MI: I should go.

She stays sitting, then stands, they are still holding hands.

EUN MI: I hope we both get in.

CHI SOO: Me too.

EUN MI walks away.

CHI SOO: Thank you for the book.

EUN MI exits, CHI SOO sits still.

SCENE FOUR

EUN MI walks down the corridor in the run down school building. CHI SOO walks after her.

CHI SOO: Eun Mi.

EUN MI carries on walking.

CHI SOO: Wait!

EUN MI walks quicker. CHI SOO runs past her, blocks her.

CHI SOO: Didn't you hear me?

EUN MI looks up and down the empty corridor.

EUN MI: I mustn't be seen with you.

CHI SOO looks at EUN MI.

CHI SOO: Are you ashamed of me?

EUN MI: … Someone saw us outside the cinema.
They told my mother.

CHI SOO: We weren't doing anything wrong.

EUN MI takes a step away from him.

EUN MI: My mother's very strict.

CHI SOO: That's why we have to work hard and get to P'yongyang.

Pause.

CHI SOO: How much longer can they keep us waiting? It was a week when we went to the cinema, it's been two weeks since … Have you been avoiding me for two weeks?

CHI SOO looks at EUN MI, she looks away.

CHI SOO: They have to tell us soon.

EUN MI looks at CHI SOO.

CHI SOO: What's that … in your eyes? Is that …? Have you heard?

EUN MI: Yes.

CHI SOO: And?

EUN MI: I got in.

CHI SOO: That's great … When did you?

EUN MI: Last week.

CHI SOO: … If they don't send a letter does that mean?

Pause.

EUN MI: I'm sorry.

Pause.

CHI SOO: Don't … if it was you. If it was the other way round I wouldn't … I promised not to pity you. You should show me the same respect.

EUN MI glances up and down the corridor.

CHI SOO: Don't you like me anymore?

EUN MI looks at him.

CHI SOO: Because you got in and I didn't?

EUN MI: I like you. You have to believe me I /really …

CHI SOO: /You aren't better than me.

EUN MI: I know. You should have got in.

CHI SOO: We're communists, we're equal.

EUN MI looks at him.

CHI SOO: Please … don't write me off. This will make me stronger. You said that … disappointment gives more depth.

EUN MI: Sadness.

CHI SOO: It feels much the same.

Pause.

CHI SOO: It's my fault.

EUN MI: No.

CHI SOO: I was arrogant, too sure of myself. I wasn't good enough. This setback is probably the best thing for me. I'm going to work harder, give up football and completely focus on acting. This will make me a better artist, a more devoted communist. Next year I'll get in.

EUN MI: No.

CHI SOO: I will get to P'yongyang.

EUN MI starts to walk away.

CHI SOO: Don't you believe in me?

CHI SOO catches hold of her arm, she stops, turns.

EUN MI: Don't you know anything? Everyone knows except you.

CHI SOO: Knows what?

EUN MI: … You have tainted blood.

Pause.

EUN MI: Where do you live?… What does your father do?

Pause.

EUN MI: My father used to do the background checks, rate people's songbun. We're not equal … There are fifty-one distinct categories that make up three main classes: core, wavering and hostile.

Pause.

CHI SOO: What are you?

EUN MI: Core … but the bottom of the core.

CHI SOO: And me?

EUN MI looks at him.

EUN MI: How can you not know?

CHI SOO: Hostile.

EUN MI: Yes.

CHI SOO: Towards the top or bottom?

EUN MI looks down.

CHI SOO: Say it. I can take it.

EUN MI: The bottom.

Pause.

CHI SOO: People in the hostile class don't get to go to P'yongyang do they?

EUN MI: No.

CHI SOO: Do they get to join the army?

EUN MI: No.

CHI SOO: Do they get to go to high school?

EUN MI: Not usually.

CHI SOO: What can I do to …?

EUN MI: … Nothing.

Pause.

EUN MI: We … the state practices three generations of cleansing. Your life will be the same as your father's … If you have children … They can't expect anything more than you or your father.

CHI SOO turns away from EUN MI.

CHI SOO: What did he do?

Pause.

CHI SOO: Please … Tell me what everyone else knows.

Pause.

EUN MI: Ask him.

CHI SOO: I will.

Pause.

EUN MI: My mother's a widow. I have a younger brother. They're both counting on me.

CHI SOO: Go.

EUN MI looks at CHI SOO.

EUN MI: I'm sorry.

CHI SOO: When did you know what people say about …?

EUN MI: At the cinema, when you were waiting for Sun Hee … I knew you'd have a spare ticket.

Pause.

CHI SOO: And that night when we were talking about going to P'yongyang together?

EUN MI: I mean't it. That's what I … wanted.

CHI SOO: You knew I wouldn't pass the audition didn't you?

EUN MI: I wasn't sure. I hoped … I hoped that if you were outstanding they'd forgive your songbun.

CHI SOO: But I wasn't.

EUN MI: They couldn't forgive it.

EUN MI glances around nervously.

CHI SOO: Go.

EUN MI hesitates.

EUN MI: Before we met. I used to sit in maths willing you to turn around and notice me … It's not that I don't like you.

EUN MI turns, walks quickly away.

SCENE FIVE

A single concrete room, bare except for pictures of Kim Il Sung and Kim Jong Il on the wall. MRS PARK cooks a stew over a single stove.

MR PARK enters, he wears the dark blue uniform of a coal miner. MRS PARK looks at him and smiles.

MRS PARK: You're back.

MR PARK: Sorry I'm late.

MRS PARK: I worry.

MR PARK: I know.

MRS PARK: Start imagining accidents.

MRS PARK stirs the stew.

MRS PARK: Gas leaks, fires, explosions, floods, mine shafts collapsing, you trapped in the dark slowly suffocating.

MR PARK walks towards MRS PARK, she takes a spoonful of the stew, blows on it.

MR PARK: I'm a very careful man.

MRS PARK holds out the spoon.

MR PARK: I've too much to live for.

MR PARK tastes the stew. Makes a sound of pure pleasure.

MR PARK: How do you make a simple stew taste like that?

MRS PARK beams.

MRS PARK: Five thousand three hundred and five.

MR PARK looks at her.

MRS PARK: Days that you've come back to me.

MR PARK: You could have had … Do you ever regret it?

MRS PARK: Marrying you? No. But I'd like to see my mother again.

CHI SOO enters, looks at his parents then turns away from them.

MR PARK: I hope you're hungry.

MRS PARK: How was your day?

Pause.

CHI SOO: Did a letter come for me?

MR and MRS PARK exchange a look.

CHI SOO: I can't bear the waiting for much longer.

Pause.

CHI SOO: If I don't get in, I don't know what I'll do.

CHI SOO turns and looks at his father.

CHI SOO: Is there something you want to tell me?

Pause.

CHI SOO: Why do we live out here in this single room?…
Why are you a coal miner?

Pause.

MR PARK: I …

CHI SOO: *(Loudly.)* What are you ashamed of?

MRS PARK: Sssh. The walls have ears.

CHI SOO: Do you think the neighbours don't know?
Everyone knows except me.

MR PARK looks at his son.

MR PARK: I was born in the south.

CHI SOO: Then I'm …

MR PARK: Yes.

CHI SOO: *(Loudly.)* Did you fight in the war?

MR PARK: Yes.

MRS PARK: Sssh please.

CHI SOO: Which side did you fight on?

MR PARK: I fought for my country.

CHI SOO: With the American bastards?

MR PARK looks at his son.

CHI SOO: I'm the son of a traitor.

Pause.

CHI SOO: You helped the evil American cunts invade
our country … They tortured millions of our people just
for fun. They ran spears through the bellies of pregnant
women, mutilated children for entertainment. A little boy
refused to shine a Yankee devil's shoes and was kicked to
death.

MR PARK: *(Softly.)* Don't believe everything they teach you.

MRS PARK: Ssh.

CHI SOO: What was that?

MRS PARK: Nothing.

CHI SOO: What did you say dog?

Pause.

CHI SOO: Traitor. I could denounce you.

MRS PARK: No. Please …

CHI SOO: You helped the American bastards destroy our
country. I've seen the photographs. They dropped bombs on
poor defenceless villages. The men were all away at the front.
When the women, children and old people ran to the fields
they were machine gunned down. Are you saying that didn't
happen?

MR PARK: No.

CHI SOO looks at his father.

CHI SOO: I wish you'd died fighting.

MR PARK holds his gaze.

MR PARK: I wished the same for many years in the gulag.

CHI SOO: Why were you ever let out? What you said …
I could send you back.

MRS PARK: No … He's still your father, your blood.

CHI SOO: *(To MR PARK.)* I hate you. If I could I'd drain
    you out of my body.

CHI SOO turns away from his father.

CHI SOO: I didn't get a letter. I didn't get in.

CHI SOO crumples like a little boy.

CHI SOO: You should have told me. Why did you let me
    audition and … hope?

MR PARK: I'm sorry.

CHI SOO: I wish I had never been born. You had no right
    to have children. No right to bring a child with no future
    into the world.

MRS PARK: You chose to come to me.

CHI SOO: No.

MRS PARK: A baby chooses it's mother.

CHI SOO: How could you choose him?

MRS PARK: Your father is a good /man …

CHI SOO: /He's a dog, less than … I'm …

MRS PARK: No … you must never believe that.

CHI SOO: If everyone says it then it … becomes truth.

Pause.

CHI SOO: Why didn't you tell me?

MRS PARK: I grew you in my body. You fed on my blood,
    took the marrow from my bones. Even when you were the
    size of a grain of rice inside me the world felt … different.
    When you were born it was just the two of us, it was long,
    difficult but I could feel your strength. The first time you
    looked at me …

CHI SOO: Why didn't you tell me?

MRS PARK: Because you were perfect. Just as good as anyone else.

MR PARK: Sssh. Careful. You were big and handsome.

MRS PARK: You rolled over early, walked early, spoke before all the other babies and in proper sentences. Every week in group criticism I confessed to feelings of pride.

MR PARK: You were born happy. We would wake up to the sound of you singing. You found delight everywhere. Do you remember when you started playing on the middle team?

CHI SOO: Yes.

MR PARK: We walked together to the match.

CHI SOO: My first proper game. Mother had made rice balls.

MR PARK: I was going to tell you then. But I couldn't tell you on the way because I wanted you to play well, to do your best. Then … I couldn't tell you on the way back because you had scored.

MR PARK is crying.

MR PARK: Despite … I hoped … I knew that today would come but I wanted to put it off for as long as possible.

CHI SOO: You let me dream … Believe that I could get the girl, that I could … be someone.

MRS PARK: We wanted you to at least have a childhood, happy memories can …

CHI SOO: Make up for no future?

Pause.

CHI SOO exits. MRS PARK reaches out to MR PARK, they hold each other.

Second Prologue

Two photographs side by side projected onto the back wall: Kim Il Sung and Kim Jong Il. A large beautifully wrapped gift on a bare stage. A hand reaches out of the gift and unties the ribbon. The gift opens like Pandora's box and EUN MI emerges. She wears a silver dress, high heels, her hair is pulled back, her lips painted scarlet.

The following ode to Kim Jong Il is to the tune of U2's 'Beautiful Day'

EUN MI: 'In the morning when the sky is aglow
                    We think of your kindly smile.
                    when the stars shine in the sky
                    We long for your warm love.'

EUN MI dances, a teasing, coy dance. When she resumes singing she is once again devoted and heart felt.

EUN MI: 'Dear Leader we honour and pledge ourselves
                    to you.
                    However violent the rain wind or blizzard,
                    Loyalty generation after generation.
                    We pledge ourselves generation after
                    generation.'

EUN MI turns upstage, drops to her knees and prostrates herself in front of the photographs.

ACT TWO

SCENE ONE

A hill by the coal mine close to a stream. MR PARK sits on the ground putting on his worn boots. CHI SOO enters wearing trousers, he is bare foot, bare chested, a threadbare towel around his shoulders, he shivers.

MR PARK: Don't you feel better for washing?

CHI SOO: I'll get filthy again tomorrow.

MR PARK: And tomorrow after work you'll wash again.

CHI SOO towels his hair vigorously.

MR PARK: The stream hasn't frozen over yet. There's still a little light. We can walk home clean men. I don't like to go home to your mother dirty.

CHI SOO: She doesn't mind.

MR PARK: I mind.

MR PARK coughs.

MR PARK: There's a pattern I've seen. Men stop washing after work, say they'll wash at home. They come to work filthy the next day. In their mind they've given up. They start drinking when they can, you can smell it on their breath. Then after a while an accident happens.

CHI SOO looks at his father.

CHI SOO: You're one of the oldest men down there.

MR PARK nods thoughtfully.

MR PARK: I've seen too many fellow workers die.

CHI SOO throws his towel down angrily.

CHI SOO: Me too.

MR PARK: One day … the anger will fade.

CHI SOO: No … It's all I have.

CHI SOO pulls on his shirt.

CHI SOO: It makes me a good worker. Every morning I wake up full of rage. I come to work, exhaust myself, like to feel the ache in my body. Go home feel empty. The anger's part of me now, it's what keeps me here.

MR PARK: That's all?

Pause.

MR PARK: That's a shame.

CHI SOO: All of this is … shame.

MR PARK: We're still … human beings.

CHI SOO: Barely.

MR PARK: I've seen people living like animals: dirty, starving, humiliated; motivated only by fear and hatred.

CHI SOO: That's us.

MR PARK: No. Down there, some of the men look out for each other. We're sitting here together, above ground, in the fresh air. We'll walk home to our supper, to your mother … She cooks the best food she can for us. If she had better ingredients we would eat like …

CHI SOO: The P'yongyang elite?

MR PARK: Yes. In our humble house we're able to live with dignity.

MR PARK gets a corncake out of a pocket and gives it to CHI SOO who eats it.

CHI SOO: Less and less corn, more like a husk cake.

MR PARK coughs.

MR PARK: In … the other place a father wouldn't do that for his son.

CHI SOO: The gulag?

MR PARK nods.

MR PARK: I wouldn't have made my quota today if it weren't for you.

CHI SOO: It's nothing.

MR PARK: It's not nothing. Thank you. In the gulag a son wouldn't do that for his father.

CHI SOO: How long were you there?

MR PARK: Ten years.

CHI SOO: Not many leave.

MR PARK: No.

Pause.

CHI SOO: How did you stay alive?

MR PARK: Every day there'd be fighting. The strong took the food from the weak. Back then I was one of the strong. But it wasn't just physical … You had to be fearless in the mind. It was much easier to die than it was to live. Most men gave up, lay down and waited … In the morning there were dead bodies crammed in amongst us. I learned more about how people function in that camp than I could have at the finest, at Kim Il Sung University.

CHI SOO glances around.

CHI SOO: Ssh.

MR PARK: My years there made me appreciate … the things that keep us human.

CHI SOO looks at MR PARK.

MR PARK: Be thankful for simple pleasures. There were
years when I dreamed of being able to wash in fresh
running water.

CHI SOO: I admire you.

MR PARK: Don't. I'm not telling you everything.

MR PARK coughs.

CHI SOO: You're steady. You keep going.

MR PARK: There's nothing else we can do.

CHI SOO: My mind … It's not as strong as yours.

MR PARK: Yes it is.

CHI SOO: No. Sometimes … it wants to give up.

MR PARK: I know.

MR PARK rests a hand on CHI SOO's shoulder.

MR PARK: But you haven't and you won't.

CHI SOO: No. I'm your son.

They look at each other in the fading light.

MR PARK: That day you found out, ran away …
When you came back you were a different person.

CHI SOO: I … everything died.

CHI SOO puts on a worn boot.

MR PARK: Then they've won.

CHI SOO: Yes they have. I'm a slave, like you. I'll wear
my rage away against the black rock until I start coughing
like you. I'll work until I die young from exhaustion …
That's it.

MR PARK looks at CHI SOO.

MR PARK: When you were a boy you used to like to read, your nose was always in a book.

CHI SOO puts on his other boot.

CHI SOO: There's no light. I wake up in the dark, come to work in the dark. When we get home it's night. There hasn't been electricity for months, not for people like us. Anyway I don't have any books.

MR PARK: That's funny. I thought I saw a book about the cinema.

CHI SOO: It doesn't belong to me. I have to give it back.

MR PARK: You used to write stories.

CHI SOO: If I had money I'd buy food not paper.

MR PARK: You used to make up stories in your head.

MR PARK coughs.

MR PARK: Your imagination, your thoughts, they're still yours. We have to be careful, can't trust anyone. But in the dark … your thoughts are your own. Everything that made you happy you … You even stopped going to the cinema.

CHI SOO: Those stories … they're not for us. Why dream about something that can't be?

CHI SOO stands up. MR PARK looks up at him sadly, stands and they both exit.

SCENE TWO

A dressing room: a dressing table with a mirror surrounded by lights, on it a vase of white roses and a bottle of Hennessy Paradis cognac. EUN MI wears an ivory silk dressing gown and silver tap shoes. She makes up her face. She stands up. Music. She practises a dance number.

She stops, lights a cigarette and smokes.

EUN MI: I have no hope. Everything I've strived for … I'll have to stay in this stinking cesspit of vice and capitalism forever … I'll never …

EUN MI blanks, she shuts her eyes and tries to remember.

EUN MI: Shit.

EUN MI goes over to her dressing table and picks up her script, reads.

EUN MI: I'll never go home. Never see the truth and beauty of Baekdu Mountain.

The intercom buzzes loudly, she presses a button.

EUN MI: Yes?

The intercom crackles.

FEMALE
VOICE: The producer would like to speak with you.

EUN MI: Yes of course … Can you tell me his name?

FEMALE
VOICE: He prefers to remain anonymous. You may call him 'Sir'.

EUN MI: … I'll need five /minutes.

PRODUCER'S
VOICE: *(Booming as if it has been amplified.)* /Hello Eun Mi.

EUN MI: Hello … sir.

PRODUCER'S
VOICE: Do you like the roses?

EUN MI: Very much. Thank you.

PRODUCER'S
VOICE: And the cognac?

EUN MI: It's too generous.

PRODUCER'S
VOICE: We have to take care of you. You're a rising
    star, a jewel of our state. Why don't you have a glass?

EUN MI: Oh perhaps later. I need to work on my lines.

PRODUCER'S
VOICE: It was flown from Paris. Have a glass.

*EUN MI searches the debris of her dressing table, finds a glass and
pretends to pour.*

PRODUCER'S
VOICE: Are you drinking?

EUN MI: Yes.

EUN MI pretends to have a drink.

EUN MI: Why can't we meet in person?

PRODUCER'S
VOICE: When I meet actresses they tend to act, to
    pretend. I value honesty. Are you honest?

EUN MI: … Yes.

PRODUCER'S
VOICE: Then break the seal on the bottle and have a
    fucking drink like I told you to.

*EUN MI looks at the mirror, opens the bottle and pours herself a
drink, she drinks, the taste is unfamiliar, she gags.*

PRODUCER'S
VOICE: I noticed you in the chorus. I suggested that
    you, a student, play a part in my birthday celebrations.
    I gave you this role. This is your big break. I can make you

into as great an actress as Oh Mee Ran or … I could finish you.

EUN MI: I'm honoured. I'm sorry.

PRODUCER'S
VOICE: What for?

EUN MI glances at the mirror.

EUN MI: … For not being grateful enough.

EUN MI slips off her stool, drops to her knees and bows.

The PRODUCER enters. He wears a grey zip up suit and oversize glasses, his hair is combed straight back. EUN MI prostrates herself. The PRODUCER sits on the chair with his legs wide open.

PRODUCER: Stand up.

EUN MI stands up. She is shaking, she keeps her eyes to the floor.

PRODUCER: Now … why don't you dance for me?

Music. EUN MI dances the tap dance she was practising earlier, she is very nervous, comes to the end, stands awkwardly.

PRODUCER: We need to work on your dancing.

EUN MI: Yes Dear Leader.

PRODUCER: You lack … sex appeal … It's not your fault. It's because you're a modest humble girl from the countryside. That's why you suit this role. Look up.

EUN MI looks up.

PRODUCER: Have you ever had feelings for a man?

EUN MI lowers her eyes.

EUN MI: … No Dear Leader.

PRODUCER: How old are you?

EUN MI: Twenty.

PRODUCER: Do you know how babies are made?

EUN MI: I … Beloved Father I'm unmarried.

PRODUCER: That's why you have no sex appeal.

EUN MI: I'm sorry.

PRODUCER: Come here.

EUN MI moves towards the PRODUCER stops just in front of him.

PRODUCER: Closer.

EUN MI moves even closer, the PRODUCER snaps his thighs together imprisoning her between them, he growls like an animal, she screams with fright.

PRODUCER: I think … with my help, we'll be able to find it.

EUN MI: Thank you Father.

PRODUCER: Sex appeal … It doesn't matter for this role but in the future … Do you understand the tone of the film?

The PRODUCER peeks inside her dressing gown with one finger. EUN MI freezes.

PRODUCER: It's a communist retelling of a Western fairytale.

EUN MI: Yes and Da Eun is an everyday hardworking heroine, she's one of the people.

The PRODUCER pulls her down so she is sitting perched on one of his thighs.

PRODUCER: Let's work on that passage you were practising.

EUN MI: I have no hope. Everything I've strived for …

The PRODUCER looks at her lips, throat.

PRODUCER: I don't believe you.

EUN MI: I have/ no.

PRODUCER: /Stop. It's hard for you because you're young and beautiful with P'yongyang at your feet … You have to imagine …

EUN MI gazes at him.

PRODUCER: You are someone who has no hope, no future.

EUN MI closes her eyes.

PRODUCER: It's as if … you worked very hard on this role and then you displeased me and I gave it to someone else, banished you from P'yongyang.

EUN MI opens her eyes.

PRODUCER: Now don't think. Just say the words.

EUN MI: I have no hope. Everything I've strived for.

PRODUCER: There … much better. I believed you that time. Go on.

EUN MI: I will have to stay in this stinking cesspit of vice and capitalism forever …

PRODUCER: No, there's not enough hatred, not enough … What's the most disgusting thing you ever had to do?

EUN MI: … Take my family's contribution of nightsoil / to the …

PRODUCER: /That's a patriotic duty.

EUN MI: But the smell …

The PRODUCER slaps her hard on the bottom, she squeaks.

PRODUCER: It's shit. And here in the DPRK even shit is put to glorious use to fertilize our fields and grow food.

EUN MI: Yes Father … I think the problem is that I've been lucky enough to grow up in the DPRK. I've never known anything but … harmony, communist perfection.

PRODUCER: Do you understand what the Emerald City represents?

EUN MI: … Seoul?

PRODUCER: Good girl.

EUN MI: Could you … describe Seoul? Then I'd understand the horror.

PRODUCER: Imagine a city of people who were once like us. But they've been infected by a virus. They have a sick relationship with America, which embodies every single vice. The relationship is like that of a weak woman with a man who beats and abuses her but she can't leave him because she's completely dependant on the scraps he throws her way. The South Koreans have no Juche. Unlike us, they weren't masters of reconstruction in their own country. They don't have the strength and revolutionary spirit of self-reliance. They have no pride in themselves and want only to imitate the Americans. Like the Americans they care only about money. They have so little self respect they even change their faces to look more Western. The city is crumbling and full of violence and depravity. Korean women prostitute themselves to American soldiers, give birth to retarded children. One day … we will save them … We are the chosen people, the saviours of the Korean race.

EUN MI: Yes Father.

PRODUCER: Da Eun believes she is trapped there forever. Can you imagine that you long to go home?

EUN MI: Sometimes … I miss my mother.

PRODUCER: If you please me … You may go home and visit your mother … Say the lines.

EUN MI: I'll never go home. Never see the truth and beauty of Baekdu Mountain.

PRODUCER: You're improving. I'm not wasting my time with you.

EUN MI slips off his thigh and sinks to the floor in a low bow. She looks up at the PRODUCER.

EUN MI: I am devoted to pleasing you. To working for the glory of the DPRK and furthering Juche ideology.

The PRODUCER looks at EUN MI's beautiful face.

PRODUCER: Then the sky maiden appears to you and tells you you've always had the power to return home. But you needed to learn that you didn't have to run away to find your hearts desire. Everything you wanted could be found right here in the Democratic People's Republic of Korea. Now … go on …

EUN MI stands up, taps her heels together.

EUN MI: There's no place like home … There's no …

The PRODUCER unties her dressing gown.

SCENE THREE

Twilight. Outside the culture hall, a poster of EUN MI on the wall. CHI SOO enters, stands looking at the poster.

CHI SOO: You did it. You made it.

Pause.

CHI SOO: What was that film we saw together?… ' We are on a turning point of youth. Everybody has the right to choose his life.'

CHI SOO laughs bitterly.

CHI SOO: More like … 'I can give you up but not my hope and dream'.

EUN MI enters, she wears black ragged hemp, stands at a distance. She gazes at the poster of herself, lights a cigarette, smokes. CHI SOO turns around.

They look at each other.

EUN MI: Chi Soo?

Pause.

CHI SOO: Congratulations.

EUN MI: Thank you.

CHI SOO: I'd like to see your film, *The Puppet Leader of the South.*

EUN MI: So would my younger brother, my friends.

CHI SOO: How long's the cinema been shut?

EUN MI: Don't you know?

Pause.

EUN MI: You used to come every week. Always managed to wrangle Sunday tickets.

CHI SOO: I don't have much time.

EUN MI: Bo Hyun says the cinema's been shut for the past year. They change the poster, that's all.

CHI SOO looks at the poster.

CHI SOO: That's some poster.

EUN MI: Thanks. It's make-up, lighting …

They look at each other.

CHI SOO: Your mourning clothes are very convincing.

EUN MI: They're not very flattering but they're a good disguise … Nice touch putting actual dirt on yours.

CHI SOO looks at her, suddenly she understands.

CHI SOO: I should go.

EUN MI: Wait. I'm sorry. Please stay … Do you want a cigarette?

EUN MI offers him a cigarette. CHI SOO stares at the foreign packaging.

EUN MI: It says Rothmans. They're from England.

CHI SOO takes a cigarette, EUN MI lights it for him.

EUN MI: Do you like it?

CHI SOO: It's alright. Kills the hunger.

EUN MI: Is it true? Are people hungry here?

CHI SOO: Some people. I'm sure your mother has enough to eat.

EUN MI: … She had a stroke.

CHI SOO: I'm sorry.

EUN MI: The Great Leader's death was too much for her. That and she's competitive, all the public outpourings of grief.

CHI SOO nods.

CHI SOO: I saw her. She was quite something. That must be where you get your acting …

EUN MI glares at him.

EUN MI: Her world has ended. She wants to die.
            Did you even cry?

CHI SOO: Yes of course. I lined up twice a day at the statue to pay my respects, at first there were rice cakes.

EUN MI: Mansudae Hill was something else … Mass hysteria. Hundreds of thousands of people crying, wailing, beating their heads on the concrete until they fainted or collapsed … I never thought the Great Leader could die.

CHI SOO: He was only a man, only human.

EUN MI: Sssh. Careful.

CHI SOO: There's no one here.

EUN MI: My mother may be out of action but there are
    a whole swarm of people lining up to take her place. Every
    single one of them would send you to the gulag to improve
    their status with the party.

Pause.

EUN MI: How are your parents?

CHI SOO: … Alive.

EUN MI: And you … how are you?

CHI SOO: … Still here.

They look at each other.

CHI SOO: Are you a movie star now?

EUN MI: No.

CHI SOO: You must be.

EUN MI: I might be a rising starlet. This is my first lead role.

CHI SOO: Tell me about your life in P'yongyang.

EUN MI: … I don't want to.

CHI SOO: Are you ashamed?

EUN MI: Yes.

CHI SOO: Me too, all the time … Please … The last time
    I came to the cinema was with you. Tonight … I don't
    know … I needed to sit in the dark and be somewhere else,
    someone else, to dream, to forget for an hour or two …

They look at each other.

EUN MI: I live in my own flat in a smart building on the
    fifteenth floor. There's a lift and a porter.

CHI SOO: Does he wear white gloves?

EUN MI: No but he wears a uniform. My flat's in the Eastern district close to the Juche tower.

CHI SOO: Where are the film studios?

EUN MI: Out in the suburbs. I used to share a flat with three girls from the chorus out there. Recently I was moved. Now a driver takes me to work.

CHI SOO: Do you eat at the revolving restaurant?

EUN MI: I have done. It's not … it isn't really the place to go anymore.

CHI SOO: Where do you go?

EUN MI: … I went to a party at the Dear Leader's palace. There was a champagne fountain.

CHI SOO: What's that?

EUN MI: A sparkling wine from France. There was more food than it was possible to eat, flown in from different countries. He has a sushi chef from Japan, two chefs from Italy. I even ate pizza.

CHI SOO: I don't know what it is.

EUN MI: A bread with cheese and dried meats.

CHI SOO: Have you met him?

EUN MI: … Yes.

CHI SOO: And?

EUN MI looks away.

EUN MI: He's … How do you describe a god? I …
I can't find the words to do him justice. I saw Sun Hee perform at his palace.

CHI SOO: I'd forgotten about her.

EUN MI: It was my mother who told her about you. She looked at me, I know she recognized me. She was dancing with a group of girls, they took their clothes off, danced naked.

CHI SOO: Slut.

EUN MI glances at CHI SOO.

EUN MI: Are you married?

CHI SOO: No. You?

EUN MI: No.

CHI SOO: I won't ever marry. Won't inflict my life on someone else.

EUN MI looks at him.

EUN MI: You were the first person who believed in me.

CHI SOO: I just thought you looked cuter when you stood up straight.

EUN MI: You told me you liked to imagine, make up films in your head. After that night … before I went to sleep I used to close my eyes and dream how my life could be.

CHI SOO: And for you it came true.

EUN MI: Nearly … When I imagined … you were with me.

CHI SOO looks at her.

CHI SOO: I'm glad you got to P'yongyang.

EUN MI: You don't hate me?

CHI SOO: No. How could I?

EUN MI: You should.

CHI SOO: No. Never.

EUN MI pulls a ballpoint pen out of her pocket, rips the silver paper from inside the packet of cigarettes, writes her address.

EUN MI: If you wanted, we could stay in touch.

CHI SOO: Why would … a film star, sorry a rising starlet want to be in touch with … someone like me?

EUN MI: The Chi Soo I knew would never have said that.

CHI SOO: We knew each other a long time ago. I was a different person then.

EUN MI: No … Underneath you're still the same.

EUN MI hands the scrap of paper to CHI SOO.

EUN MI: There's always a way to get what you want.

CHI SOO gives a dismissive sigh.

EUN MI: You said that.

CHI SOO takes the silver paper.

EUN MI: Goodbye.

CHI SOO: Goodbye.

EUN MI exits. CHI SOO stands watching her leave.

SCENE FOUR

The single concrete room. MR and MRS PARK sit at a low table.

MRS PARK: I'm tired.

MR PARK: I know.

CHI SOO enters, he carries a single sheet of paper and a worn down stub of pencil. MRS PARK ladles soup into bowls.

MR PARK: Delicious. Do you remember the dinners mother used to cook. She'd cobble together feasts, invite all our neighbours.

CHI SOO indicates towards the right wall.

CHI SOO: Did they ever invite us back? Only a fool would share food.

CHI SOO walks over to the right wall.

CHI SOO: *(Loudly.)* Thank you Respected Father Leader for our food for which we are truly grateful.

CHI SOO sits down at the table. MRS PARK ladles more soup into CHI SOO's bowl.

CHI SOO: Look. I even have a dandelion.

CHI SOO eats. MRS PARK smiles.

CHI SOO: Only mother could make a soup of salt and grass taste this good.

MRS PARK notices the paper.

CHI SOO: What is it?

MRS PARK: Why did you buy paper when you could have bought your family corn?

CHI SOO: You're right.

CHI SOO pushes his bowl of soup violently away.

CHI SOO: And I let you give me your share.

MRS PARK: I'm not hungry.

CHI SOO: Your skin's flaking, there are marks around your eyes.

MRS PARK moves the bowl back in front of CHI SOO.

CHI SOO: I'm sorry. I should have bought corn.

MRS PARK: Next time. Please eat.

CHI SOO eats. MR PARK looks at him.

MR PARK: Something's … different.

CHI SOO: No.

MR PARK: There's … a lightness about you.

CHI SOO: I'm on a strict diet of grass soup.

MR PARK: Not everything is physical. You have hope.

CHI SOO: If I do I'm …

Pause.

CHI SOO: I … bumped into someone. A girl I used to know.

MR and MRS PARK smile.

CHI SOO: She's out of my reach.

MRS PARK: The paper …

CHI SOO: She's a movie star. She's in P'yongyang.

MR PARK considers this.

MR PARK: Write her a story, for the movies. Something sad and romantic that will make her cry.

CHI SOO: Her life … she smokes English cigarettes, eats meat and cheese from Italy. Why should she cry?

MR PARK: Because you will move her.

CHI SOO: No. I can't …

MR PARK: Then don't. Give up.

MRS PARK falls forwards onto the table. MR PARK helps her up.

MR PARK: Tired?

MRS PARK: Umm.

MR PARK: Do you want to lie down. Rest?

MRS PARK looks at MR PARK.

MRS PARK: I'll sit outside. The fresh air will do me good, wake me up a little.

MR PARK helps MRS PARK up. She looks at CHI SOO, exits.

CHI SOO: At night I hear her moaning.

MR PARK: She has stomach cramps … There's nothing I can do. The streets are full of people begging for food.

MR PARK coughs.

MR PARK: I'll give you a story.

MR PARK clears his throat.

MR PARK: … There was a young man: handsome, confident. He had great fun chasing after only the prettiest girls. He lived a charmed life but then something terrible happened … Use your imagination you can make this bit up. It turned out he wasn't who he thought he was. He was only a miner, a coal miner.

CHI SOO looks at his father.

MR PARK: He worked hard for little reward, six days a week. He lived in darkness. He lost his hope and came to believe this was his life until he coughed and died.

CHI SOO: Well this is utterly depressing.

MR PARK: Wait … One day he saw a woman and she looked back at him and in her eyes he saw kindness.

Pause.

MR PARK: He had suffered; life had almost broken him. Somehow he was still alive but that kindness nearly undid him. She saw through the dirt and his uniform, saw the man he used to be. She gave him hope. Which can be a dangerous thing. Because if you hope you have to dare.

Pause.

MR PARK: Our hero, because now he is a hero again, dared to believe that the woman might not find him hideous and low. He sought her out, they talked and when he was with her he felt … content, that there was a warm place for him in the world. The heroine wasn't only kind, she had a strength of character, backbone. Her family were in the wavering class and didn't see past the dirt and low songbun. When she told them she wanted to marry the coal miner they cut her off.

CHI SOO: Oh …

MR PARK: The hero and heroine were at peace in their humble home despite their lowly jobs.

MR PARK coughs.

MR PARK: They blocked out the rest of the world and found pleasure in each other. They had a beautiful baby boy and knew … happiness. They understood the outside world would eventually judge and condemn the child but the parents shielded him for as long as possible.

MR PARK looks at CHI SOO.

MR PARK: There was a famine. The heroine made traps out of buckets and string, hung up nets. She put meat on the table, made delicacies of rats, mice, sparrows, frogs. She was kind and shared her knowledge, soon all the animals were gone. She walked to the woods, stripped the inner bark of the pine trees, spent hours grinding it into flour. Our family ate cake. Again she shared her knowledge and now the pine trees are stripped bare. This morning she got up before five to walk to the fields to pick newly grown weeds and grasses because they're easier to digest.

CHI SOO: She even found a dandelion.

Pause.

MR PARK: Think your film star can measure up?

CHI SOO: I don't know. I hope …

MR PARK: Then stay alive.

MR PARK stands up and exits. CHI SOO sits still, then starts to write.

SCENE FIVE

EUN MI's apartment: a sofa, a drinks trolley and a large flat screen television. MIN, thirty, sits on the sofa. She wears fashionable clothes and a lot of make up, a large Chinese knock-off Chanel bag by her feet.

EUN MI enters, she wears an elegant dress, looks at MIN in surprise.

MIN: Where have you been?

EUN MI: I … How did you get in?

MIN: The porter let me in. He's an old friend.
    The Dear Leader's on his way.

MIN looks critically at EUN MI.

MIN: Those won't do.

MIN fetches a pair of high heels. EUN MI changes her shoes.

MIN: Where were you?

EUN MI: I walked down Reunification Street.

MIN: … Why?

EUN MI: I don't know … I wish I hadn't.

MIN gets make-up out of her bag, applies blusher to EUN MI.

MIN: Well … I'm sure it isn't the first execution
    you've seen.

EUN MI: No … I saw her film.

MIN: An actress was executed?

EUN MI: No, Han Soon Hee. Her life story inspired *Traces of Life* … I saw it years ago … I've never forgotten it.

MIN applies red lipstick to EUN MI.

EUN MI: I read that the Dear Leader was moved to tears
    by the film.

MIN holds a tissue up to EUN MI's lips.

MIN: Blot.

EUN MI blots her lips.

MIN: Did a lot of people turn out for her?

EUN MI: There were crowds lined up all along the street.
She was accused of being a spy.

MIN: Then she must have been.

EUN MI: The man she was executed with was blamed
for the Arduous March.

EUN MI pours herself a glass of cognac, drinks.

MIN: Then he certainly got what he deserved.

MIN styles EUN MI's hair.

EUN MI: When she was brought out … there was
silence. She couldn't walk, her legs dragged … She tried to
speak through a loudspeaker but her mouth couldn't form
words. They tied her to a stake: ropes around her head,
chest and legs. She lost control of her bladder. They shot
the rope around … her head exploded, blood splattered on
the people at the front … They shot the rope at her chest,
then legs, she bowed down.

MIN: I never go to executions. Can't stomach them.

EUN MI: Afterwards … No one cheered. Do people
really believe she was a spy? That that old broken man was
/responsible …

MIN: /Yes. Everyone believes. Only stupid people
ask questions.

The PRODUCER enters.

MIN: You have a good life, plenty of opportunities,
but everything can change. Learn from her. She was once a
favourite of …

EUN MI notices the PRODUCER. Sinks to the floor in a low bow. MIN follows EUN MI's example. MIN melts into the background. EUN MI stands up.

PRODUCER: You look a little nervous my dear.

EUN MI: I'm overwhelmed with happiness to see you.

The PRODUCER looks at EUN MI.

EUN MI: How long have you been standing there?

PRODUCER: I'm everywhere. I can read your thoughts.

Pause.

EUN MI: Then you must know how much I missed you …. I think I might be … addicted to you.

EUN MI moves seductively towards him.

PRODUCER: Even though I'm as small as a midget's turd?

EUN MI freezes, glances desperately at MIN who keeps her eyes down.

EUN MI: You're not …

PRODUCER: Careful. I hate being lied to.

EUN MI: … You aren't as small as a midget's turd, but possibly the size of a normal sized person's one.

A terrifying silence before the PRODUCER starts to giggle.

PRODUCER: But it's enough to satisfy you?

EUN MI: Father … You do much more than satisfy me. I think about you all the time. Think about what we do together.

PRODUCER: Filthy girl.

EUN MI kisses him.

PRODUCER: You've been drinking.

EUN MI: Cognac, like you taught me.

The PRODUCER looks at her coldly.

PRODUCER: Why don't people have the balls to tell me the truth?

MIN gives the PRODUCER a glass of cognac, he takes it, ignores her. MIN exits.

PRODUCER: Simple and accurate that's what I want nothing more. Have you heard of Ernst Kaltenbrunner?

EUN MI: No Dear Leader.

PRODUCER: He was the only Nazi with the guts to tell Hitler the truth. Now why don't I have a Kaltenbrunner? Not even family … Especially not family … I had a younger brother …

EUN MI: Had?

PRODUCER: He drowned.

EUN MI: I'm so sorry.

PRODUCER: Are you?

EUN MI: Yes. I have a younger brother too. /I'm imagining
…

PRODUCER: /Two? But you're not a triplet.

EUN MI: No Father.

PRODUCER: Good. All triplets are taken away by the state at birth. I believed him. That astrologer told me the truth. Do you know that only a triplet can assassinate me? It's … well it must be the truth why would anyone make up something as mad as that. She's ill you know.

EUN MI: I'm sorry.

PRODUCER: Are you? If she weren't you might not be here. Certainly I wouldn't be here with you. Mee Ran had the most perfect tits, Korean tits, smallish. If I feel like something more voluptuous I send for a … Now those

perfect tits are killing her. I've flown in the best doctors,
drugs, she needs more drugs.

The PRODUCER is crying. EUN MI stares at him in shock.

EUN MI: Is Oh Mee Ran ill?

The PRODUCER knocks her on the head with his knuckles.

PRODUCER: You're a bit slow. Cancer, she has cancer.
I have new ambitions for our film industry. We need to move
forwards, we need new actors, new directors, different ways
of seeing. A Danish director won the Grand Prix at Cannes,
he's part of an avant-garde movement. It's exciting they're
taking film back to the basics back to simple storytelling
and acting. It's like the French New Wave all over again.
Why hasn't the DPRK produced a Truffaut, a Godard or a
Von Trier? I've sunk enough fucking money into the studio.
Idiots … I'm surrounded by idiots, they second guess me,
don't tell me the truth. They can all go for a long stay in the
mountains. Everything's going to change. Everyone I can't
trust has to go. This is a new era. Do you understand?

EUN MI: Yes Dear Leader.

PRODUCER: I want our films to take their rightful place on the
world stage. To be in competition at Cannes, Berlin, Venice,
Toronto, P'yongyang. Mee Ran is indisposed, I need a new
leading lady.

The PRODUCER looks at EUN MI.

PRODUCER: Do you think that might be you?

EUN MI: Only if it pleased you.

Pause.

PRODUCER: I have something for you.

The PRODUCER pulls a letter out of his pocket.

PRODUCER: It's falling apart. Cheap paper … Now who would you know who would write on paper made from corn husks?

EUN MI swallows nervously.

EUN MI: /I've been …

PRODUCER: /Anyone would think you had a secret lover. Do you?

The PRODUCER looks at her, opens the envelope.

PRODUCER: You can't hide anything from me.

The PRODUCER reads the letter.

PRODUCER: Your mother thinks you should be more grateful.

EUN MI: My mother?

EUN MI bows low to the floor.

EUN MI: I can't thank you enough for what you've done …

The PRODUCER hands her the letter.

PRODUCER: Read it. Out loud.

EUN MI reads.

EUN MI: 'I am in the best hospital in the North. The doctors know I am someone of great importance. I hope our Dear Father still visits you often. You must remember there are many actresses in P'yongyang and men love variety.'

EUN MI glances at the PRODUCER.

EUN MI: 'You must do whatever it takes to maintain his interest. Change your hair, experiment with different clothes and make-up. You mentioned *(Softly.)* disgust. Your …

PRODUCER: What was that?

EUN MI: *(Softly.)* disgust.'

PRODUCER: Louder.

EUN MI: 'Disgust. Your feelings do not come into this. Your job is to serve the Dear Leader; nothing he asks you to do is wrong. You must anticipate his desires, go even further, never deny him anything.'

PRODUCER: You should listen to her. Go on.

EUN MI: 'Your little brother.... must get to P'yongyang, get into Kim Il Sung University despite his grades.'

PRODUCER: People have been executed for less.

EUN MI prostrates herself on the floor.

PRODUCER: How dare she have such ambition?

EUN MI: She has faultless songbun. She's been a devoted member of the workers party her entire life. So was my father.

PRODUCER: She's the mother of a whore.

The PRODUCER walks around EUN MI, kicks her skirt up over her bottom.

PRODUCER: Here you are. The breadwinner. The family's opportunity.

EUN MI: She brought us up as loyal Communists, to serve the State and work for the glory of the DPRK.

PRODUCER: Turn over.

EUN MI turns over. His foot hovers in the air so she cannot sit up, she lies on her back her skirt up. The PRODUCER kicks her legs apart.

PRODUCER: I love ambition … in an actress.

The PRODUCER unzips his flies.

SCENE SIX

A train station. CHI SOO enters, counts coins in the palm of his hands.

CHI SOO: *(Calling out.)* Come on father.

CHI SOO stands, waits.

CHI SOO: What are you doing?

CHI SOO looks offstage.

CHI SOO: Don't touch … leave it alone.

MR PARK enters, he is bent over and very slow.

MR PARK: We should bury these bodies too.

CHI SOO: No father we don't know these people.

MR PARK: It's not right. They'll become wandering ghosts.

CHI SOO: Someone will come and take them away.

They walk.

CHI SOO: At least mother died at home. We were able to bury her properly.

MR PARK: She's waiting for me.

CHI SOO: No. She's at peace now. We were happy on that hill. Do you remember we used to fly our kite there?

MR PARK: Why do they all come here to die?… I want to go home.

MR PARK coughs, stops.

CHI SOO: We're going to eat noodles and meat.

MR PARK: How?

CHI SOO: There's a woman here with meat.

MR PARK: Where?

CHI SOO: Behind the station, near the tracks.

The sound of hundreds of little birds chattering.

MR PARK: If she has meat why isn't she out front?

CHI SOO: It's black market meat.

MR PARK: What sort of meat? I haven't seen any animals in …

CHI SOO: I don't know. Probably from China.

MR PARK: We can't afford it.

CHI SOO: We can.

MR PARK: How?

CHI SOO: I sold mother's shoes.

MR PARK coughs.

MR PARK: I'm tired.

MR PARK sits down.

MR PARK: Oh … a boy came round with a message for you.

CHI SOO: When?

MR PARK: Yesterday or the week before, it's all the same.

CHI SOO: What did he say?

MR PARK: … Not to write to … the girl. It's dangerous … Is it too late?

CHI SOO: No. I'm buying food not a stamp.

Pause.

MR PARK: This meat … I don't believe it exists.

CHI SOO: I've tasted it.

MR PARK: What did it taste like?

CHI SOO: … Chicken.

MR PARK: We ate chicken at our wedding, white rice, sweet potato noodles … She could do wonderful things with tofu, her fried pumpkin was the best in Komusan, no in all of Hamgyong province …

MR PARK coughs.

MR PARK: Once she even managed to get hold of oysters.

CHI SOO: What are they?

MR PARK: Meat … a muscle that tastes of the sea. I loved the sea, the sound of it, the smell of it. I used to swim every day … when I was a boy.

The sound of hundreds of birds chattering is slowed down and spaced out. It is the high pitched chatter of children. MR PARK looks at a group of starving street kids.

MR PARK: Look at that little boy.

CHI SOO: No.

MR PARK: He's filthy, half naked, no shoes just plastic bags on his feet. He doesn't look more than five. He's all that's left of his family … When was he last cared for? Fed? Look at him.

CHI SOO looks at the child.

CHI SOO: I doubt he'll last the night. There are hundreds, thousands just like him.

CHI SOO looks at MR PARK.

CHI SOO: You can't afford pity. That's how people die. Come on.

CHI SOO pulls at MR PARK's arm.

MR PARK: I can't. I'm tired.

CHI SOO: Then wait here.

CHI SOO exits. MR PARK sits staring at the group of street kids. He hums 'Half-Moon', a South Korean children's song.

CHI SOO returns carrying a bowl of noodles.

MR PARK: How much did you get for mother's shoes?

CHI SOO: Thirty won.

CHI SOO sets the bowl down in front of MR PARK.

MR PARK: I know what it is.

CHI SOO: No you don't. Not for sure.

MR PARK: I've seen too much not to believe it.

CHI SOO: Don't think. You can't afford the calories. You have to eat.

MR PARK: No.

MR PARK coughs.

CHI SOO: Your skin's flaking, you have marks around your eyes, like mother … You're dying.

MR PARK: I know.

CHI SOO glances around.

CHI SOO: *(Softly.)* Don't you want to go home? To the South? I'm going to get us out. A broker's going to help us. He knows the best route. You need to be stronger. We have to cross the river. I can't carry you.

MR PARK: Why would a broker help us?

CHI SOO: You're a South Korean soldier. A war hero. The South Korean Goverment will give you money. Lots of it.

Mr Park looks up at CHI SOO.

CHI SOO: We'll be rich. We'll eat three meals a day.

MR PARK: Take me back to our house, where you were born, where your mother died. I want to die at home.

CHI SOO: You're all I have left. You can't die.

MR PARK: I'm sorry … I'm tired. Want to rest in the earth with your mother.

MR PARK pushes the noodles towards CHI SOO.

CHI SOO: I won't die … I feel sick but I will … keep it down. If I vomit I'll scrape it off the floor and eat it again …

MR PARK: Please …

CHI SOO looks at his father and starts to eat.

MR PARK: *(Loudly.)* Go south, you have family there.

CHI SOO: Ssh.

MR PARK glances around.

MR PARK: *(Softer.)* There's no one around apart from the dead and the kochebi's. Neither are going to report us. I was born in Jangho Village in Gangwon province.

CHI SOO: What's it like?

MR PARK: A fishing village. A close community. We were poor, the Japanese took everything but they were the enemy and we looked out for each other. The water was emerald green, there were rockpools and hidden coves. My brother and /I used to …

CHI SOO: /Is he still alive?

MR PARK: I don't know. If he is, he will help you.

CHI SOO: What's his name?

MR PARK: Park Chi Soo. Your grandfather was a fisherman. When the North attacked /the South …

CHI SOO: /What?

MR PARK: We had just started working on the boats.

CHI SOO: They attacked us.

MR PARK: No.

MR PARK coughs.

MR PARK: It was summer, when the Korean People's
      Army invaded the South. Three days later they were in
      Seoul and my brother and I were soldiers … You've been
      lied to all your life.

CHI SOO: Sshh.

MR PARK: I'm not scared anymore. Won't be silenced.
      We fought together for our country.

CHI SOO: You were captured.

MR PARK: Yes.

CHI SOO: And my uncle?

MR PARK: I asked after him in the camp but … nothing.
      I kept myself alive. I thought of home … When I imagine
      heaven it's like Hanguk.

CHI SOO: Then live. Come with me.

MR PARK: Bury me next to your mother, on the hill,
      in exile.

CHI SOO looks at his father.

MR PARK: After the armistice, there was a prisoner
      exchange. We were loaded onto trains at P'yongyang
      station. I looked for him, he wasn't there. We were all
      soldiers from the South, starving, diseased, infested with
      lice and maggots. I thought I was going home. I sang …
      We went north to the mines.

Pause.

MR PARK: I'm in your blood, your bones.

CHI SOO: Yes father.

MR PARK: You'll never be rid of me.

CHI SOO bows to his father.

MR PARK: Stay alive. Go south. Go home.

SCENE SEVEN

EUN MI's apartment. She is lit by the television and watching the final scene from Titanic, she is crying. Celine Dion starts singing.

The intercom buzzes loudly. EUN MI turns off the television, presses the intercom button.

EUN MI: Yes?

MALE VOICE: A visitor is on their way up.

EUN MI: Is it our Dear Leader?

The crackle of the intercom. EUN MI panics, puts on her high heeled shoes, fusses with her hair. MIN enters. EUN MI is relieved. She turns the television back on. Celine Dion resumes singing.

MIN: Turn it down, half the building can hear.

EUN MI: Sorry.

EUN MI turns the sound down.

MIN: Don't send me to the mountains.

MIN glances at her.

EUN MI: It feels good to cry. I've never seen anything like it …

EUN MI lights a cigarette.

EUN MI: I know how Rose felt. She met someone who made her believe in herself.

EUN MI stands up, paces.

EUN MI: Even though she's American, I felt that I was Rose. What wouldn't I give to play a part like that?

MIN looks at her.

EUN MI: I've been taught to hate them but I admire the Americans for making that film. The look of it, the sets and costumes … they must have different cameras too … They can't all be evil. They must have heart and humanity to tell such a beautiful story.

MIN: You need to be careful, especially/ now.

EUN MI: /All our films are like history lessons. I get so excited when I'm sent a new script but they're all dry, didactic, about when we fought the Japanese. It's 1997 can't we make something modern, relevant to life today?

MIN: What scripts have you read recently?

EUN MI: I haven't, not …

EUN MI looks at MIN.

EUN MI: Why haven't I been sent any scripts?

Pause.

EUN MI: *Heroine of the Arduous March* was cancelled. I've got nothing lined up.

MIN: When did he last visit you?

EUN MI looks at MIN, then goes to the telephone, picks it up, dials.

MIN: You're too late.

EUN MI: Nonsense. Hello. This is Eun Mi. I'd like to speak to Our Great Sun of the Twentieth Century … Oh umm yes if he could call me back and could you … tell him *(Softly.)* I miss him … *(Loudly.)* I miss him … Thank you.

EUN MI hangs up.

71

EUN MI: It's fine. He'll call me back. Next time I see him … I'll do everything right, charm him, win him over again. Did you bring more films?

MIN searches in her bag brings out a dvd (A book falls out onto the floor.) hands it to EUN MI who stares at it.

EUN MI: *Coffee Prince*. It's written in Korean.

EUN MI stares at the cover.

EUN MI: They don't look like Koreans I've ever seen.

MIN: It's a television drama from the South. It's a comedy.

EUN MI: What's that?

MIN: It's funny, you're supposed to laugh.

EUN MI stares at MIN in incomprehension. She looks down and sees the book, it's The Art of Cinema, she picks it up.

EUN MI: Where did you get this?

MIN: I told you, I'm a border girl. I have friends who can get things from China.

EUN MI: No. This book.

MIN: Oh …

EUN MI: It's mine. It used to belong to me.

MIN: A strange man's been hanging around outside your building.

EUN MI: Is he tall, handsome?

MIN: … He looks rough, not like someone from P'yongyang. I noticed him yesterday. When I came this evening he asked if I knew you? Gave me this book to give to you.

EUN MI stands up.

MIN: I only took it so he'd leave me alone.

EUN MI goes towards the door. MIN blocks her.

MIN: You mustn't be seen talking to him.

EUN MI: He's … family.

EUN MI forces MIN out of her way, exits.

MIN: I … I told the porter to watch out for him.

MIN follows EUN MI.

SCENE EIGHT

Exterior of the apartment building. CHI SOO stands in the shadows looking up at the lights.

EUN MI runs outside.

EUN MI: *(Softly.)* Chi Soo? *(Louder.)* Chi Soo?

CHI SOO: *(Softly.)* Over here.

EUN MI sees him, walks towards him. She stops a little way away from him.

They look at each other.

EUN MI: What are you doing here?

Pause.

CHI SOO: I … I came to give you this.

CHI SOO takes a tattered sheet of paper out of his pocket, gives it to EUN MI.

EUN MI: Thank you.

An awkward silence. EUN MI starts to read the letter.

CHI SOO: Wait.

She looks at him.

CHI SOO: Read it later. When I'm gone.

EUN MI: You came all this way to give me a letter?

CHI SOO: I got your message, that it wasn't safe. I'd already … I would never put you in danger. It's a story I wrote for you.

Pause.

EUN MI: I know how hard it was for you to get here.

CHI SOO: It was all I thought about. But now … standing outside your building, looking up at the lights. Seeing all the rich, important people coming and going … I feel … foolish.

EUN MI: No.

They look at each other.

EUN MI: I'm happy to see you.

CHI SOO: Don't make fun of me …

EUN MI: I'm not. I think about you.

EUN MI moves towards him.

EUN MI: Do you remember when we used to dream of coming to P'yongyang together?

CHI SOO: Yes.

EUN MI: Well … Here we are.

CHI SOO: Here we are.

EUN MI: Is it like you imagined?

CHI SOO: P'yongyang might be but I didn't imagine myself hiding in the shadows, people looking at me like I'm a vagrant.

EUN MI: Sorry.

CHI SOO: It isn't your fault. I came straight here. Haven't exactly been able to take in the sights.

CHI SOO grins.

EUN MI: I've just had a mad idea.

EUN MI looks at him.

EUN MI: Please don't take this the wrong way.

CHI SOO: OK.

EUN MI: You could come upstairs.

CHI SOO: To your flat?

EUN MI: Yes.

CHI SOO: What about your porter?

EUN MI: … I'll have to find a way to sneak you through. You can wash in my bathroom. I'll send Min out to find you some suitable clothes and then we'll go to the restaurant at the top of the Yanggakdo Hotel.

CHI SOO: The one that turns around?

EUN MI: Yes.

CHI SOO: On it's own island?

EUN MI: Yes.

EUN MI giggles.

EUN MI: You'll eat bulgogi.

CHI SOO: White rice and naengmyun. Three different types of kimchi.

They look at each other and grin. CHI SOO looks down.

CHI SOO: Is it very expensive?

EUN MI: I'll pay.

CHI SOO looks at her.

EUN MI: Don't you understand? Everything I have is down to you. If it wasn't for you I never would have passed that audition. Please … let me take you for dinner.

CHI SOO: Alright.

MIN runs out of the building.

EUN MI: Min, this is my … cousin, Chi Soo. He's come to visit.

MIN: Well I hope he has papers. The porter called the police, they're on their way.

MIN turns to CHI SOO.

MIN: Do you have a P'yongyang visa?

CHI SOO: No.

MIN: Then I suggest you start running.

CHI SOO: *(To EUN MI.)* We … we won't see each other again.

MIN: That's probably for the best.

They stand looking at each other.

CHI SOO: I'll always think about you.

EUN MI: I'll think about you too.

CHI SOO darts towards EUN MI, kisses her.

CHI SOO: Goodbye.

CHI SOO exits. EUN MI stands in a daze. MIN gives her a sharp slap on the cheek.

EUN MI: Ow.

MIN: You have no idea do you?

MIN looks at her angrily.

MIN: *Heroine of the Arduous March* wasn't cancelled, you were replaced.

EUN MI: Oh.

Pause.

EUN MI: Who by?

MIN: Does it matter?

EUN MI: I'd like to know.

MIN: Jin Ri ... I tried to warn you.

Pause.

EUN MI: How could I have been so stupid?... Even my mother tried to ... I was happy, relieved when he came to visit me less ... You don't know what he made me ...

MIN: I do. Women talk to their hairdressers. I've styled all the stars.

EUN MI: Have you done her hair? Jin Ri's?

MIN nods.

EUN MI: What's she like?

Pause.

MIN: /Clever ...

EUN MI: /Oh don't answer. I already know: pretty, ambitious, overwhelmed by our Father's attention ...

EUN MI looks at MIN.

EUN MI: There's something else isn't there?

MIN: The porter likes you. You always spoke to him, asked about his family ... He said to keep your money somewhere safe, hide as many valuables as you can. Officials will be around in the morning.

EUN MI: Am I being rehoused?

Pause.

EUN MI: Where will I be moved to?… A single room on the outer circle of … Will I even stay in P'yongyang?

MIN: I don't know.

EUN MI: I'll never get another lead role will I?

MIN: Probably not.

EUN MI: I'll go back to being in the chorus, playing bit parts if I'm lucky … It's all over …

The sound of a police siren approaching in the distance.

MIN: Come inside.

EUN MI: Yes … I have to pack … hide my …

MIN: There is something else you might want to consider.

EUN MI: What?

MIN: Let's talk inside.

EUN MI follows MIN into the building.

SCENE NINE

The single concrete room. CHI SOO packs his few possessions in a knapsack. He stands and looks around the room, it is completely bare. A sound from outside. CHI SOO freezes.

A knock. CHI SOO darts behind the door. Another knock. CHI SOO pulls out a knife.

EUN MI enters, she is dressed in black hemp, carries a bag. She looks around the bare room.

EUN MI: Too late.

CHI SOO drops the knife. EUN MI turns. They look at each other. CHI SOO walks towards her.

Tentatively, awkwardly they reach out to each other. Hold each other.

EUN MI pulls away, takes a hard-boiled egg out of her bag, gives it to CHI SOO who peels it and eats it. She hands him an orange, he looks at it in wonder, takes a bite.

EUN MI:　　No. You have to peel it.

EUN MI takes the orange and peels it, hands it to him. He tastes it, makes a sound of pure pleasure.

CHI SOO:　　This is the best thing anyone's ever given me.

They smile at each other.

EUN MI:　　I read your story. It was beautiful, made me cry.

CHI SOO:　　It's my parent's story.

EUN MI looks around the bare room.

EUN MI:　　Are they …

CHI SOO:　　Dead.

CHI SOO looks at her in her mourning clothes.

CHI SOO:　　Your mother?

EUN MI:　　Dead.

CHI SOO:　　We're both orphans.

They look at each other.

EUN MI:　　You look tired.

CHI SOO:　　I haven't slept in weeks. I'm frightened I won't wake up. That's what happened to my mother and my father.

Pause.

EUN MI:　　I see you … I see you as you really are.
The way your mother saw your father.

CHI SOO: You … you made me hope. I kept myself alive in case … you came back.

They look at each other.

CHI SOO: I'm not the boy you met at school. I've … done things.

EUN MI: Me too.

CHI SOO: I'm tall, need a lot of calories. Why don't you ask how I'm still alive?

EUN MI: Whatever you've done … I've done worse.

CHI SOO: No.

EUN MI: Whatever you did, you did to eat.

CHI SOO: I …

EUN MI puts her hand over CHI SOO's mouth.

EUN MI: Don't tell me. Lets not tell each other.

CHI SOO nods. EUN MI takes her hand from his mouth.

EUN MI: I forgive you and you have to forgive me.

CHI SOO: Yes.

EUN MI glances at the knapsack.

EUN MI: *(Softly.)* Are you going somewhere?

CHI SOO: … No.

EUN MI: I've been watching Chinese pirate dvds. I saw an American film about … a girl from the core class who … loves a man in the hostile class. They're kept apart but they think about each other, want to be with each other anyway.

CHI SOO: Fools.

EUN MI: Why?

CHI SOO: That doesn't happen. Not in real life.

EUN MI: There's always a way to get what you want.

They look at each other. They talk quietly.

EUN MI: Your story could be a movie but not in the DPRK.

CHI SOO looks at her.

CHI SOO: Why would you go anywhere else? You have everything here.

EUN MI: Not anymore.

CHI SOO: What happened?

EUN MI: Men can be fickle.

CHI SOO: I'm not.

EUN MI: The producer who cast me got bored, wanted to work with other actresses.

CHI SOO: I'm sorry.

EUN MI: It's forcing me to …

EUN MI looks at him.

EUN MI: I've seen television dramas from Seoul. All my life, I've felt sorry for the South Koreans, thought they were poor, backward, starving.

CHI SOO: No. That's us.

EUN MI: When I watched the opening sequence of *Coffee Prince* I went numb. They're like us but taller, brighter somehow. Their hair is cut in styles I've never seen. They wear clothes in different colours and textures. They're all rich … in the streets were rows and rows of cars.

CHI SOO: They have enough to eat.

They look at each other.

EUN MI: That's the life I want.

CHI SOO: Me too … I have family in the South.

EUN MI: I want to be an actress in Seoul. I want to play in comedies, in television dramas and films. You could write scripts.

CHI SOO: Do you remember when we dreamed of going to P'yongyang together?

EUN MI: Yes. We can go … together.

CHI SOO: Tonight.

EUN MI: I can't. I need …

CHI SOO: I have to leave tonight. I don't trust my neighbours. I thought you were the bowibu.

EUN MI indicates towards the left and then the right wall. CHI SOO indicates towards the right wall.

CHI SOO: They're not in.

EUN MI: Where are you crossing?

CHI SOO: Near Onsong. It's been dry for weeks, the water's low. Come with me.

EUN MI: My mother's funeral is the day after tomorrow. I have to bury her.

CHI SOO: I understand.

EUN MI: Are you using a broker?

CHI SOO: No … I met one, but he lost interest after my father died … None of them want to help men, only women. I'm going alone.

EUN MI: And then, in China?

CHI SOO: I'll meet you.

EUN MI: Yes.

CHI SOO: I'll need to find work, earn some money. Then we'll travel across China. We'll walk through the Gobi Desert at night, the stars will guide us. When we've crossed the border into Mongolia we'll give ourselves up.

EUN MI looks at him.

EUN MI: Min has connections in China, can get us papers. You met her remember?

CHI SOO: Do you trust her?

EUN MI: I think so. Why?

CHI SOO: There are terrible stories about North Korean women in China.

EUN MI: I trust her. I'm sure she's getting a cut. We'll fly to Seoul together.

CHI SOO: Fly?

EUN MI: The people she knows can get us a Chinese ID and passport.

CHI SOO: For me too?

EUN MI: Yes. I can leave in three days. Are you sure you can't wait?

CHI SOO: I have to cross tonight. They saw me selling the rest of my things in the market.

EUN MI: That …

CHI SOO looks at EUN MI.

CHI SOO: I need money. They know my father was a South Korean soldier, that both my parents are dead and nothing's keeping me here.

EUN MI: I can leave in three days. Meet me across the border in Yanji.

CHI SOO: Where in Yanji?

EUN MI: … Apparently there's a cold noodle place called Mina Shi. It's on Aidan Road by the north bus station. It has a red door and is next to a coffee shop.

CHI SOO: Mina Shi, Aidan Road, north bus station.

EUN MI: Meet me there in the evening in four days time.

EUN MI searches through her pockets, pulls out notes, gives them to CHI SOO.

EUN MI: If you can wait I can give you more.

CHI SOO: I can't.

EUN MI pulls cartons of cigarettes out of her bag.

EUN MI: For bribes.

CHI SOO: Thank you.

EUN MI: Good luck.

CHI SOO: You too.

CHI SOO reaches out and touches her face. They move closer.

They kiss, it's awkward like a teenage kiss, a first kiss.

They look at each other, embarrassed but full of feeling.

They kiss again, they get the hang of it, the kiss becomes more passionate.

EUN MI: We belong together.

CHI SOO: Yes.

EUN MI: You're my family now.

CHI SOO looks at her.

CHI SOO: If we're in South Korea we could have a baby.

EUN MI: … Yes.

CHI SOO: It wouldn't be like … He or she could have a future.

EUN MI: We'd have to be married. If we had a baby.

CHI SOO: We'll be married. I mean if you want to.

EUN MI: I want to. I love you.

CHI SOO looks at her, the words are unfamiliar to him.

CHI SOO: I love you.

CHI SOO kisses her, touches her breast. EUN MI pulls away.

EUN MI: Not like this. Four nights. We'll check into a hotel in Yanji.

CHI SOO: Yes.

EUN MI: We'll be together. We'll be safe.

EUN MI takes a candle out of her bag, lights it.

EUN MI: Go. I'll stay here until the candle burns down.

CHI SOO picks up his knapsack.

CHI SOO: There's never been anyone else.

Pause.

EUN MI: Four nights.

CHI SOO: I'll be there.

CHI SOO exits. EUN MI stands alone in the middle of the room.

ACT THREE

K-pop music plays.

A cafe in Seoul in the Hongdae area. A waitress stands behind the counter. EUN MI sits at a table drinking a cup of coffee.

CHI SOO enters. He looks at EUN MI, she looks up. He walks towards her, has a noticeable limp.

They look at each other. CHI SOO sits down.

CHI SOO: What are you drinking?

EUN MI speaks in a different accent.

EUN MI: A decaf vanilla skinny soy flat white.

She passes him a menu.

EUN MI: At first all the choice … It terrified me. I didn't know how to choose things. It would take me twenty minutes to order a beverage.

EUN MI looks at CHI SOO.

EUN MI: You look different.

CHI SOO: You too.

Pause.

EUN MI: We're older.

CHI SOO: Yes.

Pause.

EUN MI: You look well. Did you find family?

CHI SOO: Yes. I have an aunt, cousins; I work for my uncle.

EUN MI smiles at CHI SOO, he doesn't smile back.

CHI SOO: He's quite a big fish, owns a holiday resort, is moving into property development. I go to an adult education centre at night.

EUN MI: *(Her accent slips.)* Then you're a success.

CHI SOO grins at her.

EUN MI: I can't seem to lose my accent.

CHI SOO: I like your accent.

EUN MI: It has to go. Then I need to update my look.

CHI SOO: Why?

EUN MI: I'm still trying to act. They don't go for the round face shape here. They like more of a small oval. I need to lose some weight. Then I'm going to get my eyelids fixed. When I've done that I have to find a manager and an agent.

CHI SOO: I see.

EUN MI: It's a lot more … complicated here.

CHI SOO: Yes it is.

Pause.

EUN MI: What did you think Seoul would be like?

CHI SOO: I… I just thought about food, what I would eat.

EUN MI: I thought it would be like *Coffee Prince* . I didn't realise … I thought I'd be able to fit in.

The WAITRESS walks over to them.

WAITRESS: Have you decided?

CHI SOO glances through the menu.

CHI SOO: Black coffee.

The WAITRESS looks at CHI SOO, nods.

WAITRESS: Anything else for you?

EUN MI: *(In her new accent.)* No, I'm fine.

The WAITRESS nods, turns to go.

EUN MI: *(In her old accent.)* Actually I'll have a sweet rice cake.

WAITRESS: Yes Miss.

The WAITRESS walks away.

EUN MI: You can see it can't you? The pity, then the embarrassment. We make them uncomfortable …

Pause.

EUN MI: Do you still write stories?

CHI SOO: I don't have any time.

EUN MI: I still think about your story, about …

CHI SOO looks at her.

CHI SOO: What about this one?

Pause.

CHI SOO: There's a man waiting in a noodle restaurant in Yanji. He spends the last of his money on the cheapest item on the menu. He's thin and dressed in rags but he's full of joy because he believes he's about to start the life he always dreamed of with the woman he loves. Every time the door opens he starts, hopes it might be her. When the restaurant closes he waits outside because she said she was coming and he believed her.

Pause.

CHI SOO: Where were you?

EUN MI: I'm sorry. I'm so sorry.

CHI SOO: What happened?

EUN MI: I couldn't cross that night. A border guard had
  been bribed. His rota was changed. I had to wait until the
  next night. There was no way to get a message to you.

They look at each other.

CHI SOO: I arrived here a year ago. I found out you'd
  been here eleven years. I thought you'd … changed your
  mind.

EUN MI: No … no … After I crossed I made them drive
  as fast as … It wasn't fast enough. I got there in the early
  morning. I hoped you might still be there.

CHI SOO: I was stupid.

EUN MI: Don't say that.

CHI SOO: I waited outside the noodle place all night.
  I was exhausted, let myself fall asleep. Woke up to a
  Chinese policeman kicking me. He made it clear that if I
  had money he would have taken a bribe but I didn't.

EUN MI: I had yuan, lots of it.

The WAITRESS walks over.

EUN MI: I must have arrived moments after …

CHI SOO: Yes.

*The WAITRESS puts the coffee and rice cake on the table, walks back
to the counter.*

EUN MI: I asked the owner if she had seen you, she said
  every North Korean fitted your description. I wanted to
  stay in Yanji, look for you. The police were on a drive to
  find runaways. It wasn't safe to stay.

CHI SOO: No.

EUN MI: When I got here … I asked after you at Hanawon, called all the North Korean networks but no one had heard of you.

CHI SOO: I was repatriated.

EUN MI: To … to a gulag?

CHI SOO: No, to Kyohwaso No. 12, a re-education camp.

EUN MI: But … you escaped.

CHI SOO: I served a five year sentence.

Pause.

EUN MI: Your limp … Is that from?

CHI SOO: Yes.

EUN MI: Tell me about it.

CHI SOO: … No.

EUN MI: Please … tell me I need to know.

CHI SOO looks at her.

CHI SOO: After I was released I went back to Komusan. I heard about your brother. I'm sorry.

Pause.

EUN MI: As soon as I got here, got through security I contacted a broker to get him out. I was too late.

CHI SOO: Do you know where he was sent?

EUN MI: Kwanliso No. 22 … He was made an example of, he's there for life.

CHI SOO: My father was in the Kwanliso, the gulag.

EUN MI: Then they let people out?

CHI SOO: Sometimes … If they can keep themselves alive.

Pause.

EUN MI: Every night I put my daughter to bed and then, find myself at my computer googling North Korean gulag, I can't stop myself. There are detailed reports about … There are line drawings of different tortures. I imagine … I read horrific stories: a woman managed to give birth to a living baby even though she was starving. A guard heard the baby's cries, he beat the mother and then forced her to hold her baby's head under water until it died. That's one of many … I think about them all the time … I'm fat and I hate myself. I can't seem to lose my babyweight. I go to the gym, drive there in my Hyundai. I have too much of everything. You're good … better than me. You waited until everyone was dead.

CHI SOO reaches out to take her hand, sees her wedding ring.

CHI SOO: I avoid other North Koreans. We all have ugly stories, something to hide.

They sit holding hands.

CHI SOO: When I was in the camp I made up stories, played them like films in my head. I imagined you walking into the noodle place. I imagined us together in a hotel room, the rest of the world shut out. I pictured myself coming to Seoul and meeting you. Whatever they did to me, I had hope, believed that somewhere far away there was love. You kept me alive. I imagined … the face of our child.

EUN MI takes her hand away, starts to cry. CHI SOO fumbles in his pocket, takes out a packet of cigarettes offers her one. She looks longingly at the cigarette.

EUN MI: I gave up.

CHI SOO puts the cigarettes back in his pocket.

EUN MI: I'm married.

CHI SOO: I know.

EUN MI: I have a baby.

CHI SOO: I know.

EUN MI: I thought you'd died.

Pause.

EUN MI: I was on my own here.

Pause.

EUN MI: The money they give you doesn't last long.
            Everything's expensive. I didn't know how to budget.
            I thought I'd get work as an actress but … I'm too old,
            I have a funny voice, the wrong face.

CHI SOO: Not to me.

Pause.

EUN MI: I wish … I hadn't left.

CHI SOO: Don't say that.

EUN MI: This isn't home.

CHI SOO: You have a child, a husband who must … care
            for you.

Pause.

EUN MI: I was approached by a television producer.
            I… I thought it was an opportunity. They were making a
            documentary about Northern women marrying Southern
            men. They wanted me to be one of the North Korean
            women, to tell my story.

CHI SOO: That's fantastic.

EUN MI: I didn't do it. My husband didn't want his
            friends and colleagues to know that I'm from North Korea.

CHI SOO looks at her.

EUN MI: He doesn't love me like you. He doesn't know
me or understand me and I don't love him the way I do
you.

Pause.

EUN MI: If only you had waited or I had given you
more money … If …

CHI SOO: No ifs.

EUN MI: We could have …

CHI SOO: Yes.

EUN MI: But not now.

Pause.

CHI SOO: I know.

*The lights turn on outside, a street full of blinking neon. CHI SOO
gazes out of the window.*

CHI SOO: All that electricity for one city. Do you ever
miss it?

EUN MI: What?

CHI SOO: The darkness. I miss the stars. I could look up
and see every single star.

Pause.

CHI SOO: Here there's all this information. Kim Jong
Il has his own private Swiss bank account: Division 39,
billions of US dollars. He forced rice farmers to grow
opium, sells heroin and methamphetamine to China and
Japan. Our people are hard workers. There's fish in our
seas. Minerals in our ground. We didn't have to be that
poor. Not so many of us needed to die.

EUN MI: I hate him.

CHI SOO: The world does … nothing, laughs, treats him like a joke. Everyone turns the other way. The South likes it's prosperity, doesn't want to share.

EUN MI: He's old now, not in good health.

CHI SOO: The regime can't last. Every foreign policy think tank is predicting it's fall.

Pause.

EUN MI: When it does. Will you go back?

CHI SOO: Yes. I'll go to P'yongyang.

EUN MI: Me too.

CHI SOO: I'll rebuild my country. I'm educating myself, we'll need people who understand business when the time comes.

EUN MI: I'll help rebuild the North Korean film industry. I'll act again.

CHI SOO: The DPRK can't last. Kim Jong Il can't last.

EUN MI: No.

CHI SOO: Your brother needs to keep himself alive, somehow get enough to eat until the prisons are opened.

EUN MI: Yes.

Sudden blackout and silence. A power cut down the entire street.

CHI SOO lights his cigarette lighter and places it on the table.

EUN MI: I'm glad we met up, that you got in contact.

CHI SOO: Me too.

EUN MI: I feel better, hopeful.

CHI SOO: You always made me hope.

Pause.

EUN MI: In the dark … we could be somewhere else.

Pause.

CHI SOO: Let's imagine the best possible outcome.

EUN MI: Yes.

Pause.

CHI SOO: Can you see it?

EUN MI: I think so.

CHI SOO: Then we have to believe that it can happen.

They sit in silence in the darkness, lit only by a single flame.

Lights down.